ONCE THEY LIVED IN GLOUCESTERSHIRE

A Dymock Poets Anthology

Linda Hart

Green Branch

ONCE THEY LIVED IN GLOUCESTERSHIRE

British Library Cataloguing-in-publication data
A catalogue record for this book is available from the British Library.
ISBN 0 9526031 52

This edition copyright © 2000 by Linda Hart

First published in 1995 by Green Branch Press, Kencot Lodge, Kencot,
Lechlade, Gloucestershire GL7 3QX, United Kingdom.
Tel. 01367 860588. Fax 01367 860765.

Printed and bound by Severnside Printers Limited, Bridge House, Upton-
upon-Severn, Worcestershire WR8 0HG

Dedicated to
my father
who introduced me to poetry
with nightly readings from
A Child's Garden of Verses
and
to all the friends I have made
through the Friends of the Dymock Poets

Contents

Acknowledgements

Graham Greene said that "Writing is for the most part a lonely and unsatisfying occupation. One is tied to a table, a chair, a stack of paper." That is true, but only up to a point. For with this project I have also been tied to a wonderful collection of books – some old, some new, some borrowed and many others that now belong to my Dymock Poets collection. And when not tied to the chair and table, I have seen, talked to and corresponded with many people in the course of preparing this anthology. My warm thanks and appreciation go to all of those listed below.

For early advice about the project, John Powell Ward.

For lending me books that helped to make this anthology possible: Roy Palmer, Roger Pope, Sean Street, Sheila and John Burns, Diana and Peter Carter, Caroline and Christopher Yapp.

For spotting and buying a crucial book for me, Sue Montague.

For obtaining books from a number of far-flung places, Carolyn Huckfield, the very helpful librarian at my local library in Ledbury.

For answering numerous enquiries on bibliographic and biographic matters, Sean Street.

For reading and commenting on particular chapters: Jeff Cooper, Richard Emeny, Roger Hogg, Penny Drinkwater Self, Edward C. Thomas and Lesley Lee Francis.

For reading and making helpful comments about the manuscript, Ann Elliott Wall.

For the charcoal drawing of May Hill, Peter Arscott.

For the maps that so clearly portray the Dymock area, Ken Johnston.

For typesetting the text on his desk-top publishing system, and making helpful design suggestions, Christopher Yapp.

For his enthusiastic support from afar, Professor Jim Armstrong from Fullerton College, California, who visited England to study the literary friendship between Frost and Thomas.

On a more official note, I am grateful to the following for permission to include certain material in this book. To Gervase Farjeon for permission to quote from *Edward Thomas: The Last Four Years* by Eleanor Farjeon; to Professor R. George Thomas for permission to quote from his biography of Edward Thomas and his edition of Thomas's collected poems; to Mrs Pam Haines for permission to quote from the articles by John Haines referred to in the bibliography; to Macmillan for permission to include the poems by Wilfrid Gibson; to the Estate of Robert Frost, editor Edward Connery Lathem and publisher Jonathan Cape for permission to include poems from *The Poetry of Robert Frost*; to Jeff Cooper for permission to include the poems by Lascelles Abercrombie. Quotes from *Selected Letters of Robert Frost* edited by Lawrance Thompson, copyright ©1964 by Lawrance Thompson and Henry Holt & Co., reprinted by permission of Henry Holt & Co. Poems by John Drinkwater are reprinted by permission of Samuel French Ltd on behalf of the John Drinkwater Estate.

FOREWORD

A golden idyll in a golden land – that might be how the Dymock story could be told if we allowed nostalgia alone to dictate to us. Certainly those last years up to 1914 seem a distillation of lost innocence, a casting out of Eden. And Dymock in springtime *is* a golden land, flowing with wild daffodils that shine out from the gentle verdancy of the meadows and woods, bright against the rich red soil that has grown not only flowers, but poets in profusion over the years before and since the first decades of the century.

But the coming together of the group we call "The Dymock Poets" is about much more than a fading sentimental dream. It is about a dynamic fellowship that played a crucial and still undervalued part in literary history. Here Lascelles Abercrombie and Wilfrid Gibson published *New Numbers*, a quarterly journal that was a platform for their work, and for that of John Drinkwater and Rupert Brooke. Here Edward Thomas and Robert Frost walked the fields and climbed May Hill and evolved a new voice for poetry.

Some of these poets have been vital to the development of poetry since. Others have been unjustly neglected, out of print for some years. This book rectifies the latter folly. But it does more than that, because it identifies poems that have – directly or indirectly – grown out of "The Dymock Experience". It is a work that focuses on an important part of what was known as the Georgian movement, should be read as a witness to that era, and will I hope reawaken the debate regarding its worth.

But it will be read too as a celebration of place and of friendship. It is a volume to put in the knapsack, to settle back with in the lee of a hedgerow, at the turn of the path, on the slopes of May Hill, on "a Malvern side" or where "two roads diverge in a yellow wood" – to savour the spirit that brought the poets to Dymock: a spirit that lingers there still. By so doing, we may recall how Edward Thomas – as the sun set on that last summer – prophesied our future presence in the place as he looked forward to a time when others would. . .

. . . through other flowers
In those fields under the same moon
Go talking and have easy hours.

Sean Street
June, 1995

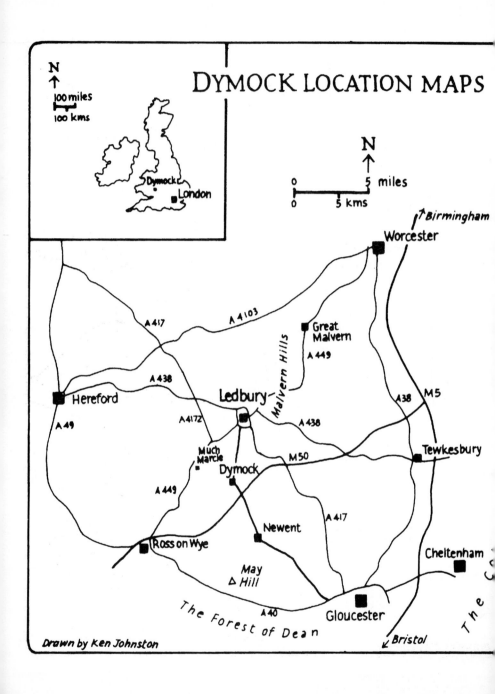

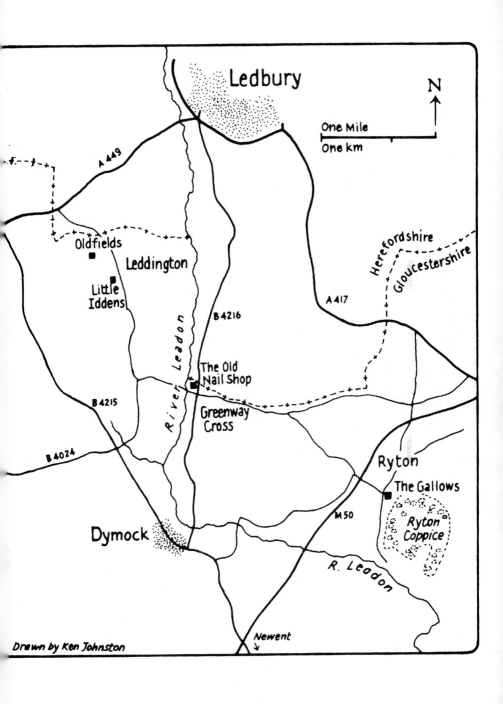

Ledbury

N

One Mile
One km

A 449

Oldfields

Leddington

Little
Iddens

River Leadon

B 4216

Herefordshire
Gloucestershire

A 417

The Old
Nail Shop

B 4215

Greenway
Cross

B 4024

Ryton

The Gallows

M 50

Ryton
Coppice

Dymock

R. Leadon

Drawn by Ken Johnston

Newent

INTRODUCTION

In the years before and during the First World War, three poets lived near the village of Dymock, in the north-west corner of Gloucestershire, and three other poets visited them for various lengths of time. These six poets – the Dymock Poets – were Lascelles Abercrombie, Wilfrid Gibson, John Drinkwater, Rupert Brooke, Robert Frost, Edward Thomas.

They did not come to Dymock as a self-conscious group – and even after their time in Dymock they would not have thought of themselves as "the Dymock Poets". But the intertwining of their lives and interests began as early as 1908, when Edward Thomas reviewed books of poems by Wilfrid Gibson and Lascelles Abercrombie. By 1912, some of the six had met each other – Brooke and Gibson, for example, meeting for the first time in September 1912. The following year they would see each other's names in the new *Georgian Anthology* that had been published by The Poetry Bookshop. Harold Monro, proprietor of the bookshop and its publishing arm, helped introduce many poets to one another. And Edward Marsh, editor of the *Georgian Anthology* and patron to many poets and artists, also thrived on making introductions.

So in 1913 the six poets would continue to meet one another through Marsh or Monro, or at the Poetry Bookshop, or through other mutual friends. By 1914 four of them – Abercrombie, Gibson, Brooke and Drinkwater – were jointly publishing a magazine of their own poetry called *New Numbers*, and two of them – Frost and Thomas – were forging a friendship to rival that of Byron and Shelley.

One of the Dymock Poets was an American, the others were English, but all of them were caught up in the immense changes taking place in post-Victorian England – changes that affected poetry as much as other aspects of life. During the years in Dymock five of the six men were in their 30s – Rupert Brooke, the youngest, was in his mid 20s. They were at different stages in their careers and their popularity – in 1912, for example, Wilfrid Gibson and Lascelles Abercrombie were popular poets with many published volumes, while Robert Frost had just arrived from America, an unknown and virtually unpublished poet, and Edward Thomas had not yet begun writing poetry.

But it was the association with a particular place that makes it possible to think of them as a group. Abercrombie moved to Dymock in 1911 and a chain of events followed over the next three years. Gibson left London and moved to Dymock, and Frost arrived shortly afterwards. Thomas began visiting the Frosts, and rented a nearby cottage in the summer of 1914. Soon, however, the war scattered them apart. But their friendships extended well beyond the time in Dymock. There were warm and frequent letters between Thomas and Frost for three years; Abercrombie and Gibson always sent each other their latest publications; Frost's poetry reading at Leeds University in 1928 was arranged by Abercrombie; in 1931 Abercrombie visited Brooke's grave on the Greek island of Skyros; and Frost came back to visit Dymock in 1957.

'The Dymock Poets' as a descriptive phrase was first used in print as the title of a magazine article by John W. Haines in the Autumn 1933 issue of *Gloucestershire Countryside*. Haines was a Gloucester solicitor with a penchant for poetry and botany. He spent time at The Gallows with the Abercrombies, met Gibson, and soon befriended Frost and Thomas. The poets corresponded with him long after the Dymock period ended, and through Haines we know a great deal about them.

Between December 1934 and February 1935 he wrote a series of long articles in the *Gloucester Journal* – one each about Gibson, Abercrombie, Frost and Thomas. Here they are referred to as "Gloucestershire poets" who were once living in "the Dymock country" or "the Leadon Valley" or "that enchanted land". Haines also gave lectures to local societies, and at least one of these was devoted to Edward Thomas.

The next attempt to keep the memory of the Dymock Poets alive was made by Dymock's former vicar, the Rev. J.E. Gethyn-Jones. He took a keen interest in local history, and in 1951 published a book about Dymock with a chapter titled 'Dymock Personalities and Poets'. With much sentimentality, some errors and occasional exaggeration he tells the story of how the six poets came to Dymock. With pride he describes the publication of *New Numbers* and its dispatch from Dymock to "the four corners of the earth. In these volumes, of fifty or sixty pages, were first printed many poems now known and loved by the entire English speaking and reading world."

He is at his best when describing the countryside that he, and they, loved:

"Here in our quiet country village they lived. They walked these lanes, these fields, these woods. They sought the first primrose on Hazards bank, the early daffodil in the coppice at Elmbridge by the Leadon stream, and, daintiest of all, the frail bluebell amongst the Ryton Firs . . . . The simple pursuits and pleasures of rural England were to them of the very essence of life, and the fragrance of a spring morning more seductive than all the perfumes of Arabia. They loved these things, and, because they loved, they wrote of them." (Gethyn-Jones, p.110)

Gethyn-Jones was a popular vicar and people in Dymock today still remember his interest in the poets. His book was crucial in establishing the Dymock Poets as a meaningful descriptive phrase and in making people realise that something of literary significance had occurred in Dymock in 1914. Gethyn-Jones's book even provided a living link with the past by recalling the names of the postmen who stamped the poets' magazine, *New Numbers*, at Dymock's post office. In the 1980s Gethyn-Jones's interest in the poets was carried on by another vicar of Dymock, the Rev. Reg Legg, who was instrumental in creating a 'Poets' Corner' in Dymock Church, where photographs and poems are on display (the exhibit is open to visitors every day of the year).

In addition to time and place, the concept of the Dymock Poets is also based on their friendships with one another. As with any group of six people, these bonds of friendship were not equal. Abercrombie and Gibson were the long-term residents who provided the geographical focus – the physical cohesion – for the Dymock Poets. Had it not been for the war they might well have gone on living there for many more years. It was Gibson and Abercrombie who provided hospitality for Brooke and Drinkwater (and there were many other visitors as well) and it was their presence that enticed Frost to the area.

Drinkwater and Brooke are linked with the Dymock Poets less through their presence in the area – they were both visitors only – and more through their involvement with *New Numbers*. But this short-lived magazine is essential to the concept of the Dymock Poets and to the sense that here was a productive poetic 'colony'. In addition, Abercrombie, Drinkwater and Brooke shared a passion for the theatre.

Frost and Thomas lived in the area – although Frost did so only for eleven months, and Thomas only for a month although he made several shorter visits. But they were not contributors to *New Numbers*. Their friendship was based on shared interests, similar personalities, and the sense that they were as close as brothers despite not having met until their late 30s. The long walks that Frost and Thomas took, the deep trust that developed, and the literary consequences are the most enticing part of the Dymock story for many people.

Various stories about the poets' time in Dymock have come down to us – in the poetry itself, in biographical accounts, and in letters. As a result we know about a happy evening at Gibson's cottage, about a supper where the poets drank too much cider, and about an encounter Frost and Thomas had with an aggressive gamekeeper. But this book is an anthology, not a history or a biography. It is time to turn to the poetry, and let it speak for itself. There are some more details about the poets in each chapter, and some background information for each poem I've chosen. The first reference to each poem that is included here is printed in **bold**

To be included in the anthology a poem had to meet at least one of the following criteria:

- refer to Dymock, the surrounding countryside or a poet's cottage in the area
- have appeared in *New Numbers*
- have been written at least partly in the Dymock area in 1911-16
- have been written about scenes, places and people in the Dymock area
- be a poem by one Dymock Poet that another Dymock Poet liked or commented on
- be a poem influenced by, inspired by or written for another Dymock Poet
- be about nature (orchards, flowers, birds, woods) or countryside people or about the war.

Only the last item in the list is a bit of a fudge, and it is applied sparingly. It is fair to say that almost every poem in this anthology is related in some way to "Dymock". This anthology helps validate the concept of the Dymock Poets by showing that there is a body of work that relates to their time in Dymock, their joint publications, and their friendships.

While doing the initial research for this book, and in the years since then, I have read some good and bad poetry, some interesting literary biographies, some fascinating letters and some serious literary criticism. Readers who want to know more about the poets and their poetry should turn to the references at the end. The trail of the Dymock Poets can be followed on the ground as well as in books – along the tracks, paths and lanes that wind between the poets' cottages (all privately owned). Large-scale illustrated maps of two waymarked routes, called Poets Path I and II, are available in local shops.

In October 1993 the FRIENDS OF THE DYMOCK POETS was formed to commemorate the Dymock Poets, and to protect the countryside between the Malverns and May Hill so that future generations can continue to enjoy it. The Friends organise social and literary events throughout the year, arrange guided walks in the Dymock Poets countryside, and publish an informative newsletter with many book reviews. Since the society began promoting the poets, Cheltenham and Gloucester College of Higher Education has opened a Dymock Poets Archive and Study Centre in Cheltenham; and six new residential streets in Ledbury have been named after the Dymock Poets. For further information send an SAE to Friends of the Dymock Poets, 7 Winston Close, Ledbury, Herefordshire HR8 2XQ.

LASCELLES ABERCROMBIE
(1881-1938)

Today Lascelles Abercrombie is the least well-known of the six Dymock Poets. Keith Clark succinctly summarised the reasons: "his verse seems turgid and wordy, his themes too metaphysical and heavy" (p.31). But Abercrombie and his work were highly admired in the early years of this century. In September 1914 Frost wrote to an American friend about him: "The fellow I am living with at present is the last poet in your Victorian Anthology. If you want to see him to better advantage you must look him up in the Georgian Anthology where he shows well in a long poem called 'The Sale of St Thomas'. Or if I can find it I will send you some time the copy of *New Numbers* containing his 'End of the World', a play about to be produced in several places – Birmingham next week, Bristol soon, and Chicago some time this winter." (Frost, p.135-6)

Abercrombie's conviction that poetry was going through an exciting period of change, and his effort to develop (in theory and practice) the concept of realism in poetry, had an important effect on subsequent literary developments. Most important, from our perspective, is that without Abercrombie there would have been no Dymock Poets. He unwittingly began the short-lived literary colony along the Leadon River in a remote corner of Gloucestershire.

Abercrombie was born in Cheshire, and attended school at Malvern College in Worcestershire – thirteen miles from Dymock. He then went to Manchester University, where he began writing poetry seriously at the age of 20. But to earn a living he worked as a clerk in a quantity surveyor's office in Liverpool where one of the partners was a family friend (Cooper). His first book of poetry, *Interludes and Poems*, was published in January 1908, and later that same year he became a journalist with the *Liverpool Courier*. Edward Thomas, when reviewing *Interludes and Poems* for the *Daily Chronicle*, wrote to Gordon Bottomley on February 26, 1908: "He is good there is no doubt . . . . [he] has his own vocabulary & a wonderful variety in his blank verse, has certainly his own vision of things, is perhaps too metaphysical . . . . I wonder what he is like & envy you your chance of knowing him." (Thomas, Bottomley, p.157-8)

"Lascelles had always wanted to live in the country," according to his grandson Jeff Cooper. In 1907 Abercrombie wrote to Catherine (who was about to become his wife) that "It is the proper thing for us . . . to be together in the country. We are not townsfolk, either of us. We belong to the earth. I do hope I shall so be able to order my life that we can live, really live, in the country." (Cooper)

It was Abercrombie's sister Ursula who made his dream come true. She and her husband were friends of Lord Beauchamp, who owned 5,000 or so acres of land around Malvern that stretched as far as Dymock (the pub in Dymock is still named The Beauchamp Arms). Ursula had become a wealthy woman when her husband died in 1907 in a riding accident. Two years later she and her second husband moved to rented accommodation at Hellens, a large 14th-century manor house in the Herefordshire countryside, just a few miles west of Malvern, where Abercrombie had been a student.

She offered to rent a nearby cottage in the village for Lascelles and Catherine, so in April 1910 they ventured south, and moved to Monks Walk Cottage in Much Marcle. Less than six months later he published his long dramatic poem, 'Mary and the Bramble', financing the venture himself. A few months later they moved to a much larger cottage – really two old cottages joined together – in the hamlet of Ryton, less than two miles as the crow flies from the village of Dymock. "The story goes," says Cooper, "that Ursula was out hunting with Lord Beauchamp one day around Ryton when she saw The Gallows empty. She asked him about it and one thing led to another until Lascelles and his family moved in almost exactly a year after moving to Much Marcle."

Here Abercrombie worked as a freelance journalist, contributing regularly to several newspapers, but he also began to turn out several major dramatic works. It was from their new home that Abercrombie published *The Sale of Saint Thomas* – which can be described as a long poem or a short play, as verse drama or dramatic verse. This was another venture into self-publishing – the first edition says on the title page:

PUBLISHED BY THE AUTHOR
Ryton, Dymock
Gloucestershire
1911

In terms of the Dymock story, the play was important for several reasons. It illustrates the 'realism' that characterised the early Georgians, and that was to gain them fame and notoriety in literary circles. There were objections to the self-conscious brutality in the play (Ross, p.127), particularly in a passage about the flies in India that I have included here. The play was also important for a more practical reason: this second experience of publishing Abercrombie's work must have given the couple the confidence, two years later, to begin publication of *New Numbers,* a quarterly magazine containing work by Abercrombie, Gibson, Drinkwater and Brooke.

The Sale of Saint Thomas was soon reprinted as Abercrombie's contribution to the new anthology of *Georgian Poetry* (December 1912). The fact that it appeared first in the volume (due to alphabetical order) only partially accounts for the play's enormous impact. Almost all the Georgians "were intent upon restoring drama to poetry. Several also attempted to restore poetry to drama." (Ross p.121) Abercrombie tried to do both. *The Nation* reviewer (March 8, 1913) noted Abercrombie's "astonishing power of dramatic psychological analysis. He is a vehement, imaginative thinker." *The Times Literary Supplement* thought his was the most important poetic talent since the turn of the century (Hassall, Marsh, p.686). Abercrombie was now a poet to be reckoned with and this must have encouraged Wilfrid Gibson, a year later, to move to a cottage a mile north of Dymock and two miles on lanes and tracks from the Abercrombies.

The admiration was mutual. Abercrombie had favourably reviewed Gibson's *Daily Bread* in 1910. And when he reviewed *Georgian Poetry 1911-1912* (in the *Manchester Guardian*, January 8, 1913) he singled out Gibson because, he said, Gibson's work illustrated better than anyone's how contemporary poetry was dealing with new themes but respecting the traditional conventions.

Abercrombie's most important review, for our purposes, was a very long and thorough one in *The Nation* (June 13, 1914) of Frost's second book, *North of Boston*. Walsh calls it "a pioneer review", based on "reasoned literary principles", the first one to evaluate seriously the sound-of-sense ideas (Walsh, p.170). John Haines sent the review to Frost, who replied from Little Iddens: "I liked it very well. The discussion of my technique wouldn't have been what it was if Abercrombie had had nothing to go on but the book. He took advantage of certain conversations in which I gave him the key to my method and most of his catchwords." But Frost recognised that "it was a generous review to consider me in all ways so seriously and as I say I liked it." (Frost, p.127)

This review, with phrases like "unique and entirely original", was reprinted in a Boston newspaper, bringing Frost's name to public attention in American literary circles for the first time. Soon after arriving back in America in 1915 he was being hailed as a successful poet. Frost realised that this was a crucial review, and wrote to Abercrombie from New Hampshire in September 1915: "Yours was the first praise over there, and there will never be any other just like it." (Frost, p.93)

When Abercrombie wasn't working, he and Catherine must have been welcoming and easy-going hosts. Frost, Drinkwater and Brooke, as well as John Haines, Eddie Marsh, and the Gloucestershire poet Ivor Gurney have all commented on the happy times they spent with the Abercrombies at Ryton. The primitive washing facilities seem to have made the place even more endearing to them. The Frost family lived at The Gallows for five months (see the chapter on Frost) and he obviously felt sentimental about his time there. A letter to Abercrombie from New Hampshire in September 1915 says "Now I should like to go out into the yard and shake hands with your big cold pump till his iron tank was as full of water as my heart is of Ryton memories." (Frost, p.193)

Abercrombie's next verse drama, *The End of the World*, had as big an impact as *Saint Thomas*. Eddie Marsh was the first to enthuse about it. On August 17, 1913 he visited The Gallows for the first time and wrote to Brooke with glowing descriptions of the bucolic scene (including the bathroom, "a shed out of doors, with a curtain instead of a door"), of how he enjoyed cutting up French beans and peeling potatoes, and of his "longish walk with L.A. – it's lovely country and we climbed a high hill. . .and he made me swill 'mild' at every pub". Abercrombie, working on *The End of the World* at this time, read the beginning of it to Marsh, who told Brooke it was "magnificent" (Hassall, Marsh, p. 241-2).

In February 1914 Marsh returned to Dymock, partly to see the newly married Gibson who was living near Abercrombie. He wrote to Brooke in Tahiti about his weekend at The Old Nailshop with "the Wilfrids who seem flawlessly happy. . . . The Lascelles dined with us on Sat. and we with them on Sunday. . . . L. read out his *End of the World*, now finished, and to appear in the 2nd *N.N.* It's a sublime work, in its fusion of poetry and comedy there has been nothing like it. . . We had a lovely walk, it's beautiful country. . . . " (Hassall, Marsh, p.268)

The following month Abercrombie went to London as Marsh's guest for five days. Again Marsh wrote to Brooke, describing the whirlwind of lunches, teas and dinners with famous people that he laid on for Abercrombie – "Lascelles almost speechless with admiration, he didn't know there *were* such people" – as well as trips to the theatre, to the House of Commons to hear Winston Churchill deliver a speech and to the Poetry Bookshop where Abercrombie did a reading from *The End of the World*. Marsh reported that "L. is rewarding me with the dedication of *The End of the World*, which will in itself assure me of immortality." (Hassall, Marsh, p.273)

The End of the World was published in April 1914, in the second issue of *New Numbers*. Brooke, sending a copy of *New Numbers* to Mrs Chauncey Wells, said: "There's some awfully good Abercrombie in it; and we're rather proud of the whole thing." (Brooke, p.593) And Frost wrote to Abercrombie shortly after his return to America, saying that he wanted to show *The End of the World* to several people and wanted some copies of *New Numbers* sent to him (Frost, p.157).

But there were criticisms of Abercrombie's play, and most of these "were directed not so much to the poet's use of realism per se as to its artistic irrelevancy and the apparently deliberate brutality of Abercrombie's conception" (Ross, p. 128). The passages about frogs being crushed under cartwheels were, said D.H. Lawrence, "nasty efforts at cruelty" (Ross, p.129). But none of the criticism stopped Marsh from reprinting it in the second *Georgian Poetry* anthology or Drinkwater from producing it for the Birmingham Repertory Theatre's 1914 season (Street, p.85).

Abercrombie, unfit for military service, left The Gallows in March 1916 to work in a munitions factory in Liverpool. But he made a return visit in 1919, staying with a friend at Crowfield Farm near Dymock, and his creative impulses, which had dried up during the war, now re-emerged. He wrote many poems, one of the finest and best known being **'Ryton Firs'**. Its theme is declared in one stark line: "Ryton Firs, like Europe, fell." The poem recalls the beautiful woods near The Gallows, felled and used as pit-props in Welsh mines. These were the woods where Frost and Thomas were walking when they were told to leave by one of Lord Beauchamp's gamekeepers. For Haines, "nothing ever written has described so well the daffodils and the 'fresh red mounded earth' of the Dymock and Redmarley country." (Haines, *Gloucester Journal*, January 12, 1935)

Abercrombie and Brooke first knew of each other when Harold Monro, editor of *The Poetry Review*, asked Brooke in September 1912 to write a defence of Abercrombie's poetry against an attack made by Ezra Pound. "I'm not so fervent an admirer of Abercrombie's as many people," Brooke told Monro, "but perhaps that's all the better, as I *do* think him good." (Brooke, p.403) Although Abercrombie had been publishing Brooke's poems in *New Numbers*, the two men didn't meet until the day after Brooke's homecoming party in London in June 1914. Brooke insisted that Abercrombie stay overnight at Marsh's so that they would have more time to talk. "I think he's very remarkable," Brooke wrote to Ka Cox (Hassall, Brooke, p.449). Soon thereafter Brooke made the first of two visits to Dymock, to see Abercrombie and Gibson in their rural hideaway and discuss the next issue of *New Numbers*.

But war broke out, Brooke became a soldier, and there were to be no more visits to Gloucestershire. Despite wartime shortages, Abercrombie and Gibson managed to produce the fourth issue of *New Numbers* which had been promised to subscribers, but all four poets agreed that this would be the final issue. Brooke was pressed to hurry up and send some poems along. In December 1914, from Blandford Camp in Dorset, Brooke wrote to Marsh: "I hear Winston's expected [to visit here]. *Insist* on coming with him. . . . I see Lascelles is lecturing on War & the Drama. How is he? Won't you bring him down with you, as Assistant Clerk, or Admiralty Bard, or something? I'd like to see him." (Brooke, Letters, p.639) From the Aegean four months later, and less than three weeks before his death, Brooke wrote a long letter to Abercrombie from his sickbed, telling him to "come and join us", inquiring after the Gibsons, and commenting on the last *New Numbers*: "I saw a notice of NN4 in the *Times*: by a laudatory half-wit. He didn't seem to realize it was 'good-bye'. Perhaps we should have put in a slip to say so; and extracted, even in these times, a few tears, a few shillings" (Brooke, p. 678). He also wrote letters ensuring that Abercrombie would receive the royalties from his book should he die in the Aegean.

Like Gibson and Drinkwater, Abercrombie wrote a poem about Brooke's death, titled '**R.B.**'. He also wrote a lengthy obituary in the *Morning Post*. The money Abercrombie received from Brooke's royalties helped him considerably, especially during the war years when there was no market for literary criticism. In 1931 Abercrombie and his wife travelled to Greece, as Abercrombie had been asked to deliver the oration when a statue of Brooke was erected on the island of Skyros. We can only wonder at his emotions, and memories of his happy times with the dazzling young man, as he stood beside Brooke's grave.

Edward Thomas was killed in the war just as Abercrombie was helping to get Thomas's poems published for the first time (see the chapter on Thomas). Thomas had heard about Abercrombie's inability to write during the war, and wrote to Gordon Bottomley from France in March 1917: "I should also like to hear that Abercrombie had either begun writing or had got over his impatience at not being able to." (Thomas, Bottomley, p.280) Less than a week before he was killed, Thomas wrote again and mentioned Abercrombie: "I hope very much to see him & new work of his some day. I do not know his equal for keenness and warmth." (Ibid p.283)

After the war Abercrombie became a respected professor, at Liverpool University, Leeds University, Bedford College (London) and Merton College (Oxford). A verse drama, called *Phoenix: Tragicomedy in Three Acts*, was published in 1923 and dedicated to John Drinkwater. He also wrote several books, such as *The Idea of Great Poetry* (1925) and *Principles of Literary Criticism* (1932). While Professor of English Poetry at Leeds University, he arranged for Frost to give a poetry reading there on his 1928 visit to England. Abercrombie received many honorary degrees and became a Fellow of the Royal Academy in 1937. In 1930 his collected poems and plays were published. With characteristic modesty and regret, he wrote in the Preface: "The invitation to collect these pieces by the Oxford University Press was one which I could not but accept with the keenest pleasure; I allowed it to overbear a certain unwillingness to bring together poems which, to me, must chiefly represent unrealized ambition."

In 1932 Abercrombie looked back wistfully on his years at Dymock:

"I have lived in a cottage in the daffodil country, and I have, for a time, done what I wanted to do . . . . and I have known what it is to have Wilfrid Gibson and Robert Frost for my neighbours; and John Drinkwater, Rupert Brooke, Edward Thomas, Will Davies, Bob Trevelyan, Arthur Ransome, have drunk my cider, and talkt in my garden. I make no cider now, and I have no garden. But once I lived in Gloucestershire."(Gawsworth, pp.20-21)

The Sale of Saint Thomas

The Sale of Saint Thomas deals with the legend of the doubting Apostle, Thomas, and his journey to India. An introduction explains that "when the Apostles sorted the countries among themselves, the lot of India fell to Thomas. After some hesitations, he obeyed the lot, being shamed thereto by his Master, as is here set forth."

This poem, originally under 600 lines, was expanded later by Abercrombie to roughly 3,000 lines and published by Martin Secker in 1930, making it, said Haines, "one of the most important contributions to English Literature in the last decade." (*Gloucester Journal*, November 12, 1935)

In this excerpt from the 1911 edition, Thomas is at the quayside talking to the captain of the ship which is to take him to India. The captain has been telling him about some dreadful things that happen in India. He has just described how the king tortured a man because he could not speak the native language.

CAPTAIN. Have you the Indian speech?

THOMAS. Not yet: it will be given me, I trust.

CAPTAIN. You'd best make sure of the gift. Another stranger,
Who swore he knew of better gods than ours,
Seemed to the king troubled with fleas, and slaves
Were told to groom him smartly, which they did
Thoroughly with steel combs, until at last
They curried the living flesh from off his bones
And stript his face of gristle, till he was
Skull and half skeleton and yet alive.
You're not for dealing in new gods?

THOMAS.   Not I.
Was the man killed?

CAPTAIN.   He lived a little while;
But the flies killed him.

THOMAS.   Flies? I hope India
Is not a fly-plagued land? I abhor flies.

CAPTAIN. You will see strange ones, for our Indian life
Hath wonderful fierce breeding. Common earth
With us quickens to buzzing flights of wings
As readily as a week-old carcase here
Thrown in a sunny marsh. Why, we have wasps
That make your hornets seem like pretty midges;
And there be flies in India will drink
Not only blood of bulls, tigers, and bears,
But pierce the river-horses' creasy leather,
Ay, worry crocodiles through their cuirasses
And prick the metal fishes when they bask.
You'll feel them soon, with beaks like sturdy pins,
Treating their stinging thirst with your best blood.
A man can't walk a mile in India
Without being the business of a throng'd
And moving town of flies: they hawk at a man
As bold as little eagles, and as wild.

The End of the World

The End of the World tells the story of a stranger (later revealed to be a dowser) who arrives at a pub in a remote valley. Although there are few clues as to the identity of the place – but note the reference to the red earth – it would be nice to think that Abercrombie had in mind a village and pub somewhere near May Hill in Gloucestershire. The stranger tells the villagers that a comet is heading towards earth and everything will be destroyed. After much discussion and the passage of time, they discover that they have been hoaxed and the dowser is "a tramping conjurer".

Excerpt One: The Stranger has been thinking and talking about the terrible and cruel things he's seen on his travels, but has not yet told them about the comet. Sollers is a wainwright. Huff is a farmer whose wife has left him to live with one of the farm labourers in the village. This has left him embittered and cynical. They are both trying to understand what the stranger is talking about.

SOLLERS. I know what's in his mind. When I was young
My mother would catch us frogs and set them down,
Lapt in a screw of paper, in the ruts,
And carts going by would quash 'em; and I'ld laugh,
And yet be thinking, 'Suppose it was myself
Twisted stiff in huge paper, and wheels
Big as a wall of a barn treading me flat!'

HUFF. I know what's in his mind: just madness it is.
He's lookt too hard at his fellows in the world;
Sight of their monstrous hearts, like devils in cages,
Has jolted all the gearing of his wits.
It needs a tough brain, ay, a brain like mine,
To pore on ugly sin and not go mad.

STRANGER. Madness! You're not far out.—I came up here
To be alone and quiet in my thoughts,
Alone in my dreadful mind. The path,
Of red sand trodden hard, went up between
High hedges overgrown of hawthorn blowing
White as clouds; ay, it seemed burrowed through
A white sweet-smelling cloud,—I walking there
Small as a hare that runs its tunnelled drove
Thro' the close heather. And beside my feet
Blue greygles drifted gleaming over the grass;

And up I climbed to sunlight green in birches,
And the path turned to daisies among grass
With bonfires of the broom beside, like flame
Of burning straw: and I lookt into your valley.
I could scarce look.
Anger was smarting in my eyes like grit.
O the fine earth and fine all for nothing!
Mazed I walkt, seeing and smelling and hearing:
The meadow lands all shining fearfully gold,—
Cruel as fire the sight of them toucht my mind;
Breathing was all a honey taste of clover
And bean flowers: I would have rather had it
Carrion, or the stink of smouldering brimstone.
And larks aloft, the happy piping fools,
And squealing swifts that slid on hissing wings,
And yellowhammers playing spry in hedges:
I never noted them before; but now—
Yes, I was mad, and crying mad, to see
The earth so fine, fine all for nothing!

Excerpt Two: Merrick is the village smith. Once the villagers see the comet in the sky, and accept that it will soon land in their valley, they begin reflecting on their lives and the meaning of life in general.

MERRICK. 'Twas bound to come sometime,
Bound to come, I suppose. 'Tis a poor thing
For us, to fall plumb in the chance of it;
But, now or another time, 'twas bound to be.—
I have been thinking back. When I was a lad
I was delighted with my life: there seemed
Naught but things to enjoy. Say we were bathing:
There'ld be the cool smell of the water, and cool
The splashing under the trees: but I did loathe
The sinking mud slithering round my feet,
And I did love to loathe it so! And then
We'ld troop to kill a wasp's nest; and for sure
I would be stung; and if I liked the dusk
And singing and the game of it all, I loved
The smart of the stings, and fleeing the buzzing furies.

And sometimes I'ld be looking at myself
Making so much of everything; there'ld seem
A part of me speaking about myself:
'You know, this is much more than being happy.
'Tis hunger of some power in you, that lives
On your heart's welcome for all sorts of luck,
But always looks beyond you for its meaning.'
And that's the way the world's kept going on,
I believe now. Misery and delight
Have both had liking welcome from it, both
Have made the world keen to be glad and sorry.
For why? It felt the living power thrive
The more it made everything, good and bad,
Its own belonging, forged to its own affair,—
The living power that would do wonders some day.
I don't know if you take me?

SOLLERS.   I do, fine;
I've felt the very thought go through my mind
When I was at my wains; though 'twas a thing
Of such a flight I could not read its colour.—
Why was I like a man sworn to a thing,
Working to have my wains in every curve,
Ay, every tenon, right as they should be?
Not for myself, not even for those wains:
But to keep in me living at its best
The skill that must go forward and shape the world,
Helping it on towards its masterpiece.

MERRICK And never was there aught to come of it!
The world was always looking to use its life
In some great handsome way at last. And now—
We are just fooled. There never was any good
In the world going on or being at all.
The fine things life has plotted to do are worth
A rotten toadstool kickt to flying bits.
End of the World? Ay, and the end of a joke.

Ryton Firs

For David, Michael, Ralph

Dear boys, they've killed our woods: the ground
Now looks ashamed, to be shorn so bare;
Naked lank ridge and brooding mound
Seem shivering cowed in the April air.

They well may starve, hills that have been
So richly and so sturdily fleeced!
Who made this upland, once so green,
Crouch comfortless, like an ill-used beast?

There was a fool who had pulled fierce faces
At his photographer thirty years;
He swore, Now I'll put you through your paces,
Jaegers, Uhlans, and Grenadiers!

Was he to blame? Or the looking-glass
That taught him his moustachioes?
How could that joke for an Attila pass?
Who was to blame? Nobody knows.

He but let loose the frantic mood
That toppled Europe down pell-mell;
It rippled against our quietude,
And Ryton Firs, like Europe, fell.

Now the axe hews, the bill-hook lops.
The owls have flown to Clifford's Mesne,
The foxes found another copse;
The badger trotted to Mitcheldean.

But where is our cool pine-fragrance fled?
Where now our sun-fleckt loitering hours,
Wading in yellow or azure or red,
Daffodil, bluebell, foxglove flowers?

Where is our spring's woodland delight
To scatter her small green fires like dew?
Our riding, a blade of golden light
Cleaving our summer shade in two?

The wind comes noiseless down the hill
That once might just have left the sea,
And would our Glostershire windows fill
With a sound like the shores of Anglesey.

The poor trees, all undignified,
Mere logs, that could so sing and gleam,
Laid out in long rows side by side
Across the sloping ground, might seem

A monstrous march of rugged brown
Caterpillars, gigantically
Over the hill-top swarming down
To browse their own lopt greenery.

The last we saw of our lovely friends!
Cannibal grubs!–Then came the wains
To cart them off; their story ends
Not upright still in the winds and the rains

(As tall trees hope to end) at sea,
In graces drest that whiter shine
Than glittering winter: no, but to be
Props in a Glamorgan mine.

So come: where once we loved their shade,
We'll take their ghost an offering now.
Here is an image I have made:
Guarini and Tasso showed me how.

    •   •   •   •   •

  Ryton Firs are alive again!
And I In the heart of them am happy once again!

All round the knoll, on days of quietest air,
Secrets are being told: if it were high wind,
And the talk of the trees as loud as roaring drums,
Still't would be secrets, shouted instead of whisper'd.

There must have been a warning given once:
'No tree, on pain of withering and sawfly,
To reach the slimmest of his snaky toes
Into this mounded sward and rumple it;
All trees stand back: taboo is on this soil.'

The trees have always scrupulously obeyed.
Not only golden with your daffodil light
Lying in pools on the loose dusky ground
Beneath the larches, tumbling in broad rivers
Down sloping grass under the cherry trees
And birches: but among your branches clinging
A mist of that Ferrara-gold I first
Loved in those easy hours you made so green.
And hark! you are full of voices now! as if
Ferrara day-dreams had come back to earth
In Glostershire, transforming to a troop
Of lads and lasses, and presently a dance,
Those mornings when your alleys of long light
And your brown rosin-scented shadows were
Enchanted with the laughter of my boys.

THE VOICES

'Follow my heart, my dancing feet,
Dance as blithe as my heart can beat:
Dancing alone can understand
What a heavenly way we pass,
Treading the green and golden land,
Daffodillies and grass.'

'I had a song, too, on my road,
But mine was in my eyes;
For Malvern Hills were with me all the way,
Singing loveliest visible melodies

Blue as a south-sea bay;
And ruddy as wine of France
Breadths of new-turn'd ploughland under them glowed.
'Twas my heart then must dance
To dwell in my delight;
No need to sing when all in song my sight
Moved over hills so musically made
And with such colour played.
And only yesterday it was I saw
Veil'd in streamers of grey wavering smoke
My shapely Malvern Hills.
That was the last hail-storm to trouble spring:
He came in gloomy haste,
Pusht in front of the white clouds quietly basking,
In such a hurry he tript against the hills,
And stumbling forward spilt over his shoulders
All his black baggage held,
Streaking downpour of hail.
Then fled dismayed, and the sun in golden glee
And the high white clouds laught down his dusky ghost.'

'For all that's left of winter
Is moisture in the ground.
When I came down the valley last, the sun
Just thawed the grass and made me gentle turf;
But still the frost was bony underneath.
Now moles take burrowing jaunts abroad, and ply
Their shovelling hands in earth
As nimbly as the strokes
 Of a swimmer in a long dive under water.
The meadows in the sun are twice as green
For all the scatter of fresh red mounded earth,
The mischief of the moles:
No dullish red, Glostershire earth new-delved
In April! And I think shows fairest where
These rummaging small rogues have been at work
If you will look the way the sunlight slants
Making the grass one great green gem of light,
Bright earth, crimson and even
Scarlet, everywhere tracks

The rambling underground affairs of moles:
Though 'tis but kestrel-bay,
Looking against the sun.'

'But here's the happiest light can lie on ground,
Grass sloping under trees
Alive with yellow shine of daffodils!
If quicksilver were gold,
And troubled pools of it shaking in the sun,
 It were not such a fancy of bickering gleam
As Ryton daffodils when the air but stirs.
And all the miles and miles of meadowland
The spring makes golden ways,
Lead here; for here the gold
Grows brightest for our eyes,
And for our hearts lovelier even than love.
So here, each spring, our daffodil festival.'

'How smooth and quick the year
Spins me the seasons round!
How many days have slid across my mind
Since we had snow pitying the frozen ground!
Then winter sunshine cheered
The bitter skies; the snow,
Reluctantly obeying lofty winds,
Drew off in shining clouds,
Wishing it still might love
With its white mercy the cold earth beneath.
But when the beautiful ground
Lights upward all the air,
Noon thaws the frozen eaves,
And makes the rime on post and paling steam
Silvery blue smoke in the golden day.
And soon from loaded trees in noiseless woods
The snows slip thudding down,
Scattering in their trail
Bright icy sparkles through the glittering air;
And the fir-branches, patiently bent so long,
Sigh as they lift themselves to rights again.
Then warm moist hours steal in,

Such as can draw the year's
First fragrance from the sap of cherry wood
Or from the leaves of budless violets;
And travellers in lanes
Catch the hot tawny smell
Reynard's damp fur left as he sneakt marauding
Across from gap to gap;
And in the larch woods on the highest boughs
The long-eared owls like grey cats sitting still
Peer down to quizz the passengers below.'

'Light has killed the winter and all dark dreams.
Now winds live all in light,
Light has come down to earth and blossoms here,
And we have golden minds.
From out the long shade of a road high-bankt,
I came on shelving fields;
And from my feet cascading,
Streaming down the land,
Flickering lavish of daffodils flowed and fell;
Like sunlight on a water thrill'd with haste,
Such clear pale quivering flame,
But a flame even more marvellously yellow.
And all the way to Ryton here I walkt
Ankle-deep in light.
It was as if the world had just begun;
And in a mind new-made
Of shadowless delight
My spirit drank my flashing senses in,
And gloried to be made
Of young mortality.
No darker joy than this
Golden amazement now
Shall dare intrude into our dazzling lives:
Stain were it now to know
Mists of sweet warmth and deep delicious colour,
Those lovable accomplices that come
Befriending languid hours.'

THE DANCE

It is known to the world what a sight may be seen
In Herefordshire and Glostershire
As soon as earth remembers how to flower;
In a flood running over the fresh of the green
The daffodils pour like a cool fire:
Keep off and mind your manners, you young man.

It is like as the morning were spread on the ground
In Herefordshire and Glostershire,
And we were dancing on the golden hour;
Such a shimmering gleam is on meadow and mound,
And giving our minds such bright attire:
Leave eyeing me so bold, you forward maid.

We will call for a sorrow to pester her, she
Who's robbing us for the market-buyer,
The crone who strips the field our dances scour;
And especially everyone spoiling our glee
With trouble of love and love's desire:
Keep off and mind your manners, you young man.

And a sorrow the farmer shall have for his spite
Who scythes at our gold before it tire,
Because the blue leaves make his mown grass sour;
And another who brings on our shining delight
The tarnishing moods sweethearts require:
Leave eyeing me so bold, you forward maid.

R.B.

Beautiful life! As air delights to find
    The white heat of a fire and to be flame,
The eager world throng'd into his glowing mind
    And flame of burning beauty there became.

All things were turned to fire in him, and cast
    The light of their transfiguring round his ways.
His secret gleamed upon us; where he past
    He shone; he brought with him a golden place.

It was the purest fire of life that shone,
    This angel brightness visiting our mould.
Life knew no way to make life lovelier,none;
    But then came Death: 'I know the way. Behold!'

WILFRID WILSON GIBSON
(1878-1962)

Today it is difficult to realise how popular Gibson was in the second decade of this century – popular for both his poetry and his personality. Brooke and Frost took to him instantly – he must have had a warm and easy-going temperament – and everyone had a good word to say about him. "I have no friend here like Wilfrid Gibson," wrote Frost to an American friend in March 1914. (Frost, p.12) Brooke affectionately called him 'Wibson' and his letters to Marsh and others are full of concern for Gibson's well-being and comments about how nice he is. D.H. Lawrence wrote to Eddie Marsh in November 1913 that "I think Gibson is one of the clearest and most lovable personalities I know." (Hassall, Marsh, p.261) John Middleton Murry, in a letter of reminiscence to Christopher Hassall, says "We quickly introduced Wilfrid to Eddie [Marsh] . . . and Eddie took to him as naturally as we had done, for his singular integrity." (Hassall, Marsh, p.216)

Around 1906 Gibson ceased writing pseudo-Tennysonian verse and began writing realistic poems in which he tried to reflect the speech of ordinary people, based on events arising out of his everyday life in Northumberland and later Glasgow. By 1912, "of all the younger English poets of the day, only one, John Masefield with his 'The Everlasting Mercy', could challenge Gibson in the matter of general popularity." (Walsh, p.155-6) Poet Laureate Robert Bridges praised his "very remarkable" contributions to *Georgian Poetry*. In 1913 Frost wrote to another friend that "He is much talked of in America at the present time. He's just one of the plain folks with none of the marks of the literary poseur about him." (Walsh, p.157)

Two volumes of Gibson's poems – *Daily Bread* (1910) and *Fires* (1912) – impressed Frost, partly for their colloquial style but also because they provided evidence that there was a market for poems about ordinary people and everyday happenings. *Daily Bread* went into a third printing in 1913 – the year when Frost's first volume was published. Gibson was thought of as a poet concerned with the problems of common humanity. Frost and others may have jokingly referred to him as "the People's Poet". After Frost and Thomas had an unpleasant encounter with a gamekeeper in the woods behind Abercrombie's house, Frost wrote to a friend that *he* would now have a better claim than Gibson "to the title of the People's Poet". (Frost, p.142)

Gibson left his native Northumberland and moved to London in the summer of 1912. He worked as assistant editor for *Rhythm*, a poetry magazine being produced by John Middleton Murry and Katherine Mansfield. His salary, small but essential for his upkeep, was paid anonymously by Eddie Marsh, and it was Marsh who introduced him to Rupert Brooke on September 17, 1912. This "proved to be one of the important moments in Gibson's life." (Hassall, Marsh, p.189) Just three days later Gibson, at Brooke's invitation, attended the very first meeting to discuss the publication of *Georgian Poetry*. In November 1912 he moved into a small room above Harold Monro's Poetry Bookshop, a couple of months before it officially opened. Here he was well-placed to become even more a part of the London literary scene.

Wilfrid Gibson had read and admired Robert Frost's *A Boy's Will* when it was published early in 1913. That August he wrote to Frost, whom he had not met, urging him to bring some of his new poems to the Poetry Bookshop. Frost did so, and Gibson wrote a poem called 'The First Meeting'. Given their subsequent reputations today, this poem reminds us that at the time Gibson was the famous poet and Frost relatively unknown. Gibson wanted Frost to meet Abercrombie, and invited him to a poetry reading that Abercrombie was giving at the Poetry Bookshop. In December 1913 Gibson was married, in Dublin, to Harold Monro's secretary Geraldine Townshend. The Gibsons spent their honeymoon at The Gallows, while the Abercrombies were away, and soon afterwards they moved to a half-timbered cottage called The Old Nailshop. It was two miles west of Abercrombie's cottage, and on the road from Dymock to Ledbury.

Gibson had already suggested to Frost that he should leave Beaconsfield and come to live near Dymock. Early in 1914 the Gibsons found a place for the Frosts and their four children to live, two miles from The Old Nailshop, on the other side of the River Leadon. Geraldine Gibson wrote to Elinor Frost on 25 February 1914 that "We have just this moment got your husband's letter saying you are coming here. We are absolutely rejoiced . . . how perfectly splendid!" (Francis, p.83) In February 1914 Marsh wrote to Brooke, after a weekend at The Old Nailshop discussing *Georgian Poetry* II, that "W. hasn't really begun writing again yet, but he soon will, he feels the stirrings." (Hassall, Marsh, p.268) When he did begin, he wrote in typical Gibson fashion about the everyday things that surrounded him, and particularly the cottage that he and Geraldine loved dearly.

'The Old Nail-Shop', published in *New Numbers* 4, is one of many poems about the cottage; it shows Gibson's sense of history and continuity as well as his sympathy with poor rural folk. But the most important poem about the cottage, for Dymock Poet aficionados, is 'The Golden Room'. It describes the scene inside, on the only night we know for sure that five of the six Dymock Poets (not Drinkwater) were together for an evening. Dedicated to his wife and published in a volume of the same name in 1927, 'The Golden Room' is less than satisfactory as a poem but it accurately catches the nuances in style and personality of the poets.

The evening in question – most likely June 24, 1914, despite the fact that Gibson later remembered it as July - is almost certainly the night referred to in Thomas's letter of June 27 (see the chapter on Thomas). Brooke had just returned from his year of travels, and wanted to see Abercrombie and Gibson about *New Numbers*; Thomas and his wife were on a short holiday, possibly getting over a period of domestic discord. The poem captures Frost's intellect and expansiveness, Thomas's shyness, Brooke's merriment; but it also captures the pain that Gibson still felt – a decade later – about how the war had ended it all. One year and two weeks after this golden evening, Eddie Marsh retreated to the attic room of Gibson's cottage to spend eight days writing his celebrated memoir of Rupert Brooke.

The Great Western Railway offered special excursions to see the wild daffodils for which Dymock and Newent were (and still are) famous. It's not surprising that Gibson wrote a poem called '**Daffodils**'. It tells of a man reminiscing about his son Jack, now off fighting "in a bloody trench" but who, 18 years ago, had enjoyed picking and sniffing the daffodils. It was published in *An Annual of New Poetry* (1917), edited by Gordon Bottomley – the same volume that contained Edward Thomas's first published poems.

Dymock's daffodils are an important feature of another poem, '**To John Drinkwater**', which makes such effective use of alliteration (Dymock, daffodils, delight, dances, dreams). Like 'The Golden Room' it blames the war for bringing an end to their idyllic world. Gibson was usually more interested in people than in his physical surroundings, and two of the poems in *New Numbers* 4 – '**Girl's Song**' and '**The Orphans**' – give an idea of why he was called 'the People's Poet' (if only in jest) by Robert Frost. Both poems end on a sad note and with a sense that poor country folk have a hard life and many burdens to bear. Their lives stand in sharp contrast to the scene depicted in '**Trees**', which was dedicated to Lascelles Abercrombie and published in *Friends*, a small volume of Gibson's poems which appeared in 1916. Here we see Abercrombie reading to the poets who are gathered under an elm tree at The Gallows.

An elm features in another poem of Gibson's, also from the Dymock period and published in the following year in *Livelihood*, another volume of Gibson poems. '**The Elm**' was inspired by the fact that an elm at The Old Nailshop *was* brought down in a storm, and Gibson mentioned this when corresponding with Frost after his return to America. I see touches of Frost in the poem – for example, the first few lines of the third stanza. But it also illustrates Gibson's constant nostalgia and his repeated use of a narrow range of themes.

Farther afield were the Malverns – providing another theme for Gibson's poetry. From 'The Ragged Stone' it's clear that he walked to the southern end of the Malverns and climbed up Ragged Stone Hill with its wonderful views of May Hill to the south and the Severn plain to the east. He may have already heard two local legends – still repeated today – about the dreadful things that would happen to those on whom the shadow of the stone outcrop fell. It's interesting to see how Gibson has related this to the shadow of the war falling on everyone.

Frost became increasingly disenchanted with Gibson in 1914. It began with Gibson's review of *North of Boston* in the August *Bookman* and the incident with the gamekeeper seemed to confirm Frost's disenchantment with his friend. In his review Gibson simultaneously commends and criticises Frost's poetry. Walsh speculates on "why Gibson should have discerned less of Frost's accomplishment than Abercrombie". He notes that Gibson and Abercrombie "must certainly have talked at length, and repeatedly, about Frost and his book" (they had seen it prior to publication). "Beyond mere obtuseness," says Walsh, "one reason for his [Gibson's] blindness may have been a burdensome tinge of jealousy, aroused by his recognition that while Frost and he were in pursuit of much the same goals, the American had reached heights of art beyond anything in Gibson's prolific output, perhaps beyond anything imagined by him as possible." (Walsh, p.176-7)

Brooke's death was a great blow to Gibson. The title page of Gibson's *Friends* (1916) is dedicated 'To the memory of Rupert Brooke', followed by an untitled poem printed in italics followed by the date, 23rd April 1915. This poem is often titled 'To the Memory of Rupert Brooke' to distinguish it from the first poem in *Friends*, a long poem titled 'Rupert Brooke'. Part III only of this second poem is included here; it describes the field of poppies at The Gallows that Brooke had noticed the previous summer. Another poem in *Friends* about Brooke's death is 'To Edward Marsh', as the sub-title makes clear. It begins with a reference to the evening of the King's Cross fire when Marsh introduced Gibson and Brooke. Another poem about Brooke, titled 'Rugby: 1917', was published in Gibson's *Neighbours* (1920). Gibson was still writing poems about Brooke in 1927; 'Skyros' was published in *The Observer* in April and an anthology of that year's best poetry reprinted it (Read, p. 271).

In 1915 Gibson published a small volume called *Battle*, containing 32 poems about the war. When reading them it is hard to believe that at this time he had not been involved personally in the war. He had poor eyesight and it wasn't until two years later that the Army accepted him for clerical work. '**Before Action**' is the first poem in the collection, but there are several others that are powerful reminders of the agony of war. Gibson always belittled his own work. So perhaps his comments in a letter to Frost about *Battle* should not be taken too seriously: "I had to publish it as I felt I must make my little protest, however feeble and ineffectual – so don't be too hard on me." (Francis, p.163)

Gibson's work was popular in America and in 1917 he went on a successful reading tour there. When he returned to England in July, the Army Service Corps finally accepted him for duties at Sydenham, near London, for the remaining twelve months of the war. His son Michael was born in 1918, and Abercrombie became his godfather. When Robert and Elinor Frost came to England again in 1928 they visited the Gibsons. This resulted in a poem called '**Reunion**', and Gibson dedicated his next book, *Hazards*, in which the poem first appeared, "To Robert and Elinor Frost". Gibson continued to publish a book of poems every couple of years or so, until 1950. And he continued to go on lecture and reading tours around Britain. But his themes and the treatment he gave them seemed increasingly superficial to the modern world. His work declined in popularity to such an extent that it is hardly known today. "I am one of those unlucky writers whose books have predeceased him," he wrote to Frost in 1939. (Francis, p.190)

It would be hard to over-estimate the significance of the Dymock period to Gibson, and the domestic bliss he found with Geraldine in their old nail-shop, facing on to an even older track called The Greenway, two miles north of Dymock. When his *Collected Poems* were published in 1926 he placed at the very front of the volume an untitled poem – printed in italics – that begins '**So long had I travelled the lonely road**'.

The First Meeting

One evening, while in my London garret,
I worked upon a piece of Northern verse
About the Border-raiders, and was rapt
In my visions of my native countryside,
As my mind rambled over starlet fells—
Catching the thud of hoofs across the heath
And watching flaring flames of burning byres—
A sudden sharp tap-tapping at the door
Startled me; and, somewhat reluctantly,
I rose and opened it: and then was told
A stranger, an American, called Frost,
Had turned up, and would like to have a word
With me. I put my manuscript aside;
And, when he was shewn in, though still my thoughts
Hung around 'Bloody Bush Edge' for a brief while,
It wasn't long before the two of us
Were chatting in a close companionship;
And I had lost the last shred of regret
That I'd been interrupted in the business
Of my comparatively inconsequential work;
As I sat listening to Frost's racy speech
And relishing his pithy commentaries
On this and that. And when, too soon he rose
To leave, I gladly took from him a sheaf
Of verse he, diffidently, handed me;
Saying he'd be obliged if I would bother
To look it through, and let him have a word
Of what I thought of it . . .
. . . Thirty-five years—
Years of disastrous and dismayed distraction -
Have passed since then; and even the old house
Within whose garret we first met, was bombed
Into oblivion in the days of war:
Yet, though the wide waste of the Atlantic severs
Two old friends, who will hardly chance to meet
Again in this world, it appears to me
Incredible to think that "North of Boston" –
A work that, with direct colloquial vigour,

Expressed the essential facts of life
While, with perceptive sensibility
Infusing them with subtle implications
Of all our human hopes and fears, that give
To its New Englanders a universal
Significance—should ever have been for me
A sheaf of unfamiliar verse; and still
Stranger that Frost, my vitalising friend,
Was ever someone I had never met—
Poems and a poet, that would seem to have been
The very inspiration of my life!

The Old Nail-Shop

I dreamt of wings—and waked to hear
Through the low-sloping ceiling clear
The nesting starlings flutter and scratch
Among the rafters of the thatch,
Not twenty inches from my head;
And lay, half dreaming in my bed,
Watching the far elms—bolt-upright,
Black towers of silence in a night
Of stars—between the window-sill
And the low-hung eaves, square-framed, until
I drowsed, and must have slept a wink. . .
And wakened to a ceaseless clink
Of hammers ringing on the air. . .
And, somehow, only half aware,
I'd risen and crept down the stair,
Bewildered by strange, smoky gloom,
Until I'd reached the living-room
That once had been a nail-shop shed.
And where my hearth had blazed, instead
I saw the nail-forge glowing red;
And, through the stife and smoky glare,
Three dreaming women standing there
With hammers beating red-hot wire
On tinkling anvils, by the fire,
To ten-a-penny nails; and heard—
Though none looked up or breathed a word—
The song each heart sang to the tune
Of hammers, through a summer's noon,
When they had wrought in that red glow,
Alive, a hundred years ago—
The song of girl and wife and crone,
Sung in the heart of each alone. . .

The dim-eyed crone with nodding head—
"He's dead; and I'll, too, soon be dead."

The grave-eyed mother, gaunt with need—
"Another little mouth to feed!"

The black-eyed girl, with eyes alight—
"I'll wear the yellow beads to-night."

The Golden Room

(To G.)

Do you remember that still summer evening
When, in the cosy cream-washed living-room
Of The Old Nailshop, we all talked and laughed—
Our neighbours from The Gallows, Catherine
And Lascelles Abercrombie; Rupert Brooke;
Elinor and Robert Frost, living a while
At Little Iddens, who'd brought over with them
Helen and Edward Thomas? In the lamplight
We talked and laughed; but, for the most part, listened
While Robert Frost kept on and on and on,
In his slow New England fashion, for our delight,
Holding us with shrewd turns and racy quips,
And the rare twinkle of his grave blue eyes?

We sat there in the lamplight, while the day
Died from rose-latticed casements, and the plovers
Called over the low meadows, till the owls
Answered them from the elms, we sat and talked—
Now, a quick flash from Abercrombie; now,
A murmured dry half-heard aside from Thomas;
Now, a clear laughing word from Brooke; and then
Again Frost's rich and ripe philosophy
That had the body and tang of good draught-cider,
And poured as clear a stream.

                    'Twas in July
Of nineteen-fourteen that we sat and talked:
Then August brought the war, and scattered us.

Now, on the crest of an Aegean isle,
Brooke sleeps, and dreams of England: Thomas lies
'Neath Vimy Ridge, where he, among his fellows,
Died, just as life had touched his lips to song.

And nigh as ruthlessly has life divided
Us who survive; for Abercrombie toils
In a black Northern town, beneath the glower
Of hanging smoke; and in America
Frost farms once more; and, far from The Old Nailshop,
We sojourn by the Western sea.

                     And yet,
Was it for nothing that the little room,
All golden in the lamplight, thrilled with golden
Laughter from hearts of friends that summer night?
Darkness has fallen on it; and the shadow
May never more be lifted from the hearts
That went through those black years of war, and live

And still, whenever men and women gather
For talk and laughter on a summer night,
Shall not that lamp rekindle; and the room
Glow once again alive with light and laughter;
And, like a singing star in time's abyss,
Burn golden-hearted through oblivion?

1925

Daffodils

He liked the daffodils; he liked to see
Them nodding in the hedgerows cheerily
Along the dusty lanes as he went by,
Nodding and laughing to a fellow—ay,
Nodding and laughing till you'd almost think
They too enjoyed the jest.
                              Without a wink
That solemn butler said it calm and smug,
Deep-voiced as though he talked into a jug—
His lordship says he won't require no more
Crocks riveted or mended till the war
Is over.
              Lord! He'd asked to have a wire
The moment that his lordship should desire
To celebrate the occasion fittingly
By a wild burst of mending crockery,
Like a true Englishman, and hang expense!
He'd had to ask it, though he'd too much sense
To lift a lash or breathe a word before
His lordship's lordship closed the heavy door.
And then he laughed. Lord! but it did him good
That quiet laugh: and somewhere in the wood
Behind the Hall there, a woodpecker laughed
Right out aloud as though he'd gone clean daft—
Right out aloud he laughed, the brazen bird,
As if he didn't care a straw who heard;
But then he'd not his daily bread to earn
By mending crocks.
                        And now at every turn
The daffodils were laughing quietly,
Nodding and laughing to themselves, as he
Chuckled —*Now there's a patriot, real true-blue!*

It seemed the daffodils enjoyed it too,
The fun of it. He wished that he could see,
Old solemn-mug, them laughing quietly
At him: but then he'd never have a dim
Idea they laughed, and, least of all, at him:
He'd never dream they could be laughing at

A butler.
      'Twould be good to see the fat
Old peach-cheek in his solemn black and starch
Parading in his pompous parlour-march
Across that field of laughing daffodils:
'Twould be a sight to make you skip up hills,
Ay, crutch and all, and never feel your pack,
To see a butler in his starch and black
Among the daffodils ridiculous
As that old bubbly-jock with strut and fuss
Though that was rather rough upon the bird!
For all his pride, he didn't look absurd
Among the flowers, nor even that black sow
Grunting and grubbing in among them now.
And he was glad he hadn't got a trade
That starched the mother-wit in you and made
A man look silly in a field of flowers.
'Twas better mending crocks, although for hours
You hobbled on—ay, and maybe for days,
Hungry and cold along the muddy ways
Without a job: and even when the sun
Was shining 'twas not altogether fun
To lose the chance of earning a few pence
In these days, though 'twas well he'd got the sense
To see the funny side of things. It cost
You nothing, laughing to yourself: you lost
Far more by going fiddle-faced through life
Looking for trouble.
            He would tell his wife
When he got home; but, lord, she'd never see
What tickled him so mightily, not she!
She'd only look up puzzled-like and say
She didn't wonder at his lordship—nay,
With tripe and trotters at the price they were,
You'd got to count your coppers and take care
Of every farthing.
          Jack would see the fun—
Ay, Jack would see the joke. Jack was his son,
The youngest of the lot: and, man-alive,
'Twas queer that only one of all the five
Had got a twinkle in him—all the rest
Dull as ditchwater to the merriest jest.

Good lads enough they were, their mother's sons,
And they'd all pluck enough to face the guns
Out at the front: they'd got their mother's pluck;
And he was proud of them and wished them luck.
That was no laughing matter—though 'twas well
Maybe if you could crack a joke in hell
And shame the devil. Jack, at least, would fight
As well as any though his heart was light:
Jack was the boy for fighting and for fun;
And he was glad to think he'd got a son
Who, even facing bloody death, would see
That little joke about the crockery,
And chuckle as he charged.
               His thoughts dropped back
Through eighteen years, and he again saw Jack
At the old home beneath the Malvern hills,
A little fellow plucking daffodils,
A little fellow who could scarcely walk,
Yet chuckling as he snapped each juicy stalk
And held up every yellow bloom to smell,
Poking his tiny nose into the bell
And sniffing the fresh scent, and chuckling still
As though he'd secrets with each daffodil.
Ay, he could see again the little fellow
In his blue frock among that laughing yellow,
And plovers in their sheeny black and white
Flirting and tumbling in the morning light
About his curly head: he still could see,
Shutting his eyes, as plain as plain could be,
Drift upon drift those long-dead daffodils
Against the far green of the Malvern hills,
Nodding and laughing round his little lad,
As if to see him happy made them glad
Nodding and laughing . . .
             'They were nodding now,
The daffodils, and laughing—yet somehow
They didn't seem so merry now . . .
             And he
Was fighting in a bloody trench maybe
For very life this minute . . .
             They missed Jack,
And he would give them all to have him back.

To John Drinkwater

You speak tonight
Of Dymock and its daffodils;
And the great audience listens with delight:
And yet, and yet,
They cannot know the ecstasy that fills
My heart to hear you—they, to whom the words
Bring only pleasure tinged with no regret.

Dymock and daffodils and days of song
Before the war had scattered us apart . . .
And still in Dymock fields the daffodils
Dance to the singing of the birds;
And once again my heart,
Awakened by your words,
Dances with them a moment—as it danced
In days of old
Entranced
In singing dreams of dancing gold,
In days of old before the world went wrong.

Girl's Song

I saw three black pigs riding
In a blue and yellow cart—
Three black pigs riding to the fair
Behind the old grey dappled mare—
But it wasn't black pigs riding
In a gay and gaudy cart
That sent me into hiding
With a flutter in my heart.

I heard the cart returning,
The jolting jingling cart—
Returning empty from the fair
Behind the old jog-trotting mare—
But it wasn't the returning
Of a clattering, empty cart
That sent the hot blood burning
And throbbing through my heart.

The Orphans

At five o'clock one April morn
     I met them making tracks,
Young Benjamin and Abel Horn,
     With bundles on their backs.

Young Benjamin is seventy-five,
     Young Abel, seventy-seven—
The oldest innocents alive
     Beneath that April heaven.

I asked them why they trudged about
     With crabby looks and sour—
"And does your mother know you're out
     At this unearthly hour?"

They stopped: and scowling up at me
     Each shook a grizzled head,
And swore; and then spat bitterly,
     As with one voice they said:

"Homeless, about the countryside
     We never thought to roam;
But mother, she has gone and died,
     And broken up the home."

Trees

(To Lascelles Abercrombie)

The flames half lit the cavernous mystery
Of the over-arching elm that loomed profound
And mountainous above us, from the ground
Soaring to midnight stars majestically,
As, under the shelter of that ageless tree
In a rapt dreaming circle we lay around
The crackling faggots, listening to the sound
Of old words moving in new harmony.

And as you read, before our wondering eyes
Arose another tree of mighty girth—
Crested with stars though rooted in the earth,
Its heavy-foliaged branches, lit with gleams
Of ruddy firelight and the light of dreams—
Soaring immortal to eternal skies.

The Elm

The wind had caught the elm at last.
He'd lain all night and wondered how
'Twas bearing up against the blast:
And it was down for ever now,
Snapt like a match-stick. He, at dawn,
Had risen from his sleepless bed
And, hobbling to the window, drawn
The blind up, and had seen, instead
Of that brave tree against the sky,
Thrust up into the windless blue
A broken stump not ten feet high. . . .

And it was changed, the world he knew,
The world he'd known since he, tip-toe,
Had first looked out beneath the eaves,
And seen that tree at dawn aglow,
Soaring with all its countless leaves
In their first glory of fresh green,
Like a big flame above the mead.

How many mornings he had seen
It soaring since—well, it would need
A better head to figure out
Than his, now he was seventy-five,
And failing fast without a doubt—
The last of fifteen, left alive,
That in that very room were born,
Ay, and upon that very bed
He'd left at daybreak.
               Many a morn
He'd seen it, stark against the red
Of winter sunrise, or in Spring—
Some April morning, dewy-clear,
With all its green buds glittering
In the first sunbeams, soaring sheer
Out of low mist.

                              The morn he wed
It seemed with glittering jewels hung. . . .

And fifty year his wife was dead—
And she so merry-eyed and young. . . .
And it was black the night she died,
Dead black against the starry sky,
When he had flung the window wide
Upon the night so crazily
Instead of drawing down the blind
As he had meant. He was so dazed,
And fumbled so, he couldn't find
The hasp to pull it to, though crazed
To shut them out, that starry night,
And that great funeral plume of black,
So awful in the cold starlight.
He'd fumbled till they drew him back,
And closed it for him. . . .
                              And for long
At night he couldn't bear to see
An elm against the stars.
                              'Twas wrong,
He knew, to blame an innocent tree—
Though some folk hated elms, and thought
Them evil, for their great boughs fell
So suddenly. . . .
                        George Stubbs was caught
And crushed to death. You couldn't tell
What brought that great bough crashing there,
Just where George sat—his cider-keg
Raised to his lips—for all the air
Was still as death . . . And just one leg
Stuck silly-like out of the leaves
When Seth waked up ten yards away,
Where he'd been snoozing 'mid the sheaves.

'Twas queer-like; but you couldn't say
The tree itself had been to blame.
That bough was rotten through and through,
And would have fallen just the same

Though George had not been there. . . .

'Twas true

That undertakers mostly made
Cheap coffins out of elm . . .

But he—

Well, he could never feel afraid
Of any living thing. That tree,
He'd seemed to hate it for a time
After she'd died . . . And yet somehow
You can't keep hating without rhyme
Or reason any live thing.

Now

He grieved to see it, fallen low,
With almost every branch and bough
Smashed into splinters. All that snow,
A dead-weight, and that heavy blast,
Had dragged it down: and at his feet
It lay, the mighty tree, at last.

And he could make its trunk his seat
And rest awhile, this winter's noon
In the warm sunshine. He could just
Hobble so far. And very soon
He'd lie as low himself. He'd trust
his body to that wood.

Old tree,

So proud and brave this many a year,
Now brought so low . . .

Ah! there was he,

His grandson, Jo, with never a fear
Riding a bough unbroken yet—
A madcap, like his father, Jim!
He'd teach him sense, if he could get
Behind him with a stick, the limb!

The Ragged Stone

As I was walking with my dear, my dear come back at last,
The shadow of the Ragged Stone fell on us as we passed

And if the tale be true they tell about the Ragged Stone,
I'll not be walking with my dear next year, nor yet alone.

And we're to wed come Michaelmas, my lovely dear and I;
And we're to have a little house, and do not want to die.

But all the folk are fighting in the lands across the sea
Because the king and counsellors went mad in Germany.

Because the king and counsellors went mad, my love and I
May never have a little house before we come to die.

And if the tale be true they tell about the Ragged Stone,
I'll not be walking with my dear next year, nor yet alone.

To the Memory of Rupert Brooke

He's gone.
I do not understand.
I only know
That as he turned to go
And waved his hand
In his young eyes a sudden glory shone:
And I was dazzled by a sunset glow,
And he was gone.

23rd April, 1915

Rupert Brooke
(Part III)

Your eyes rejoiced in colour's ecstasy
Fulfilling even their uttermost desire,
When, over a great sunlit field afire
With windy poppies, streaming like a sea
Of scarlet flame that flaunted riotously
Among green orchards of that western shire,
You gazed as though your heart could never tire
Of life's red flood in summer revelry.

And as I watched you little thought had I
How soon beneath the dim low-drifting sky
Your soul should wander down the darkling way,
With eyes that peer a little wistfully,
Half-glad, half-sad, remembering, as they see
Lethean poppies, shrivelling ashen grey.

To Edward Marsh

(In memory of Rupert Brooke)

The night we saw the stacks of timber blaze
To terrible golden fury, young and strong
He watched between us with dream-dazzled gaze
Aflame, and burning like a god of song,
As we together stood against the throng
Drawn from the midnight of the city ways.

To-night the world about us is ablaze
And he is dead, is dead . . . . Yet, young and strong,
He watches with us still with deathless gaze
Aflame, and burning like a god of song,
As we together stand against the throng
Drawn from the bottomless midnight of hell's ways

10 June 1915

Skyros

(Rupert Brooke: April 23, 1915)

Skyros—he spoke the name
With eager, boyish zest
And little guessed
His heart should come to rest
For evermore on that far island crest.

Skyros—I heard the name,
Nor ever thought 'twould be
Aught else to me,
Nor how unrestingly
My heart should haunt that far Aegean Sea.

Skyros—to me by day
An isle of marble white
Transfused by bright
Raptures of singing light
A beacon-fire of living song by night!

Before Action

I sit beside the brazier's glow,
    And, drowsing in the heat,
I dream of daffodils that blow,
    And lambs that frisk and bleat—

Black lambs that frolic in the snow
    Among the daffodils,
In a far orchard that I know
    Beneath the Malvern hills.

Next year the daffodils will blow
    And lambs will frisk and bleat;
But I'll not feel the brazier's glow,
    Nor any cold or heat.

Reunion

To Robert Frost

Without, the October chestnuts' still gold flame;
Within, the lively flicker of the logs
Of the first Autumn fire, as once again
We sit beside the hearth—the four of us

Who once were nine, and by another hearth
Than that we knew of old in Gloucestershire
Before war overwhelmed our world and scattered,
As sparks before the wind, our little circle
Of friendly spirits broadcast . . .
                              Fourteen years
Of silence lie between us—fourteen years
The windy wilderness of the Atlantic
Has severed us with wave on wandering wave
Of ever-changing changelessness ; and we,
Over whom time's waves have washed, and who are left
Changed to the world and to each other's eyes
Maybe—are we, too, not unchanged at heart ?

Disastrous years have had their way with us
Terrors and desolations and distresses,
That put a sudden period to our youth
Just when our powers were ripening, left us aged
Before our time: yet now we sit at peace
Talking once more together, as we talked
With Abercrombie, Brooke and Thomas then
Of the old craft of words.
                              We talk of words,
And pause, and talk again, and pause ; and they
Are with us in the silences, our friends,
The absent living and the living dead . . . .

The hour of parting nears : and soon once more
The windy wilderness of the Atlantic
Will separate us, for how long, who knows ?

Yet, though we meet no more, what wave shall ever
Divide old friends whose faith is Solomon's,
Singing defiance of the many waters ?

6 October 1928

So long had I travelled the lonely road

So long had I travelled the lonely road,
Though now and again a wayfaring friend
Walked shoulder to shoulder and lightened the load
I often would think to myself as I strode—
No comrade will journey with you to the end.

And it seemed to me, as the days went past
And I gossiped with cronies or brooded alone
By wayfaring fires, that my fortune was cast
To sojourn by other men's hearths to the last
And never to come to my own hearthstone.

The lonely road no longer I roam:
We met, and were one in the heart's desire:
Together we came through the wintry gloam
To the little old house by the Greenway home
And crossed the threshold and kindled the fire.

The Old Nail-shop,
The Greenway,
1914.

JOHN DRINKWATER
(1882-1937)

Of the six Dymock Poets, JohnDrinkwater was the most versatile as an artist. He was a poet, playwright, essayist, anthologist, actor, theatre producer and director, in addition to his day-to-day job as manager of Barry Jackson's Birmingham Repertory Theatre – described by Drinkwater as "the most distinguished playhouse in the country" when it opened in February 1913 (Drinkwater, *Discovery*, p. 232). He gradually got to know each of the Dymock Poets in turn, although his connections with Frost and Thomas seem fairly inconsequential.

Drinkwater grew up with a deep passion for the countryside of Warwickshire, Worcestershire and Oxfordshire (Drinkwater, *Inheritance*, chaps 32 to 35). He left Oxford High School at 15 and worked at an insurance company in Nottingham. The hours were long and the work tedious, but he read widely and began to write poetry. When the firm moved him to Birmingham at the turn of the century he became involved with amateur dramatics, which he had always loved. In 1910 he left his job to work with Barry Jackson and The Pilgrim Players – one of the provincial repertory companies popular at this time.

Drinkwater's first book, *Lyrical and Other Poems*, was published by Harold Monro's Samurai Press in 1908 (also Gibson's publisher at the time). Drinkwater's second volume, *Poems of Men and Hours*, was published by David Nutt in 1911. This is the same publishing house that produced Frost's first volume of poetry, *A Boy's Will*, in 1913. Frost's grand-daughter thinks that Drinkwater may well have been the unknown reader who advised Mrs Nutt to accept Frost's manuscript containing the poems that became *A Boy's Will* (Francis, page 211).

In 1911 Drinkwater became president of the Birmingham Dramatic and Literary Club, and met many artists and writers as a result. He began corresponding with Gibson at this time about the possibility of producing a dramatic poem from Gibson's *Daily Bread*. Gibson didn't travel to Birmingham to see the performance nor the production a few months later of another dramatic poem of his. In fact, Gibson soon decided that he was "not much drawn to the theatre as a medium of expression. I know this is heresy nowadays," he confessed to Drinkwater (Drinkwater, *Discovery*, p.214). But Drinkwater loved the theatre, and spent the rest of his life writing plays, directing them and performing in them.

But it was poetry that led to his meeting with Abercrombie. After reading a laudatory but unsigned article in *The Nation* about a book of his poems,

Drinkwater made some inquiries and learned that Abercrombie was the reviewer. This "greatly added to my pleasure in the praise, as I knew and greatly admired his *Interludes*" (Drinkwater, Discovery, p.218). So Drinkwater wrote and introduced himself to Abercrombie, and in May 1911 he made the first of many visits to The Gallows. "I was enchanted by it and by my first sight of Gloucestershire landscape, but most by meeting the poet whom I so much admired. . . . I had been working hard and was tired, but I sat into the night with a delighted sense of refreshment." Unfortunately they drank a good deal of "mulled cider liberally laced with rum" and during the night Drinkwater woke the Abercrombies and announced that he was about to die (Drinkwater, Discovery, p.211).

In September 1912 Drinkwater invited Gibson (whom he had never met) and Abercrombie to visit him in Birmingham. "The visit was, for us all I think, a memorable success," recalled Drinkwater, "and lifelong attachments sprang from it" (Discovery, p.216). "Between Wilfrid Wilson Gibson, Lascelles Abercrombie, and myself there was from the first a bond of affectionate understanding. We really liked each other's work, and took pleasure in saying so. I thought that they were among the best poets of their time, as I still do, and I hoped to see them adding power to the revival of poetic drama in the theatre which I then thought was coming." (Discovery, p.213)

In 1912 Drinkwater was asked by Middleton Murry and Katherine Mansfield to contribute to *Rhythm* (later called *Blue Review*). He saw Harold Monro on his visits to London, wrote frequently for *The Poetry Review* and was invited by Monro to Eddie Marsh's meeting in September 1912 to discuss the idea of an anthology of contemporary English poetry. This became *Georgian Poetry*, and Drinkwater, along with Gibson and Abercrombie, were regular contributors. At this meeting Drinkwater met Brooke for the first time (three days after Brooke had met Gibson for the first time). Brooke was "then the most noted young man in London," according to Drinkwater. They left the meeting together, and walked to Holborn, with Brooke promising to send Drinkwater his book of poems. (Drinkwater, Discovery, p.228)

When Brooke sent Drinkwater *Poems 1911* he wrote that he was "feeling much excited" about the new repertory work in Birmingham (Drinkwater, p.20). Brooke's great interest in the theatre must have added to the intellectual attraction between these two men. Brooke had been deeply involved with the Marlowe Dramatic Society at Cambridge, and was working on *John Webster and the Elizabethan Drama* when he met Drinkwater. This 30,000 word essay, a fine piece of literary criticism still cited as an authoritative work today, won Brooke a Fellowship to King's in March 1913. That same month he visited Drinkwater in Birmingham; "we stayed up most of the night talking," says Drinkwater. In

May, just before his trip to America, Brooke sent Drinkwater a play he had written called *Lithuania*. Drinkwater attended the reunion supper for Brooke when he returned from his travels abroad in June 1914, and later Brooke went to Birmingham where, recalls Drinkwater, "we exhausted the complete theory of drama in a tea-shop, went to a Promenade Concert afterwards, and again talked till morning. Also he arranged to take Lascelles Abercrombie, Wilfrid Gibson, and myself in a motor-car to some quiet place where we could discuss *New Numbers*." (Drinkwater, p.20-21) But the trip never took place.

With war threatening in the early summer of 1914, Brooke and Drinkwater managed to meet a couple of times for lunch in Soho, and Drinkwater recalls "the note of foreboding. . . that seemed to touch all his words thereafter till the end." (Drinkwater, p.21) When Brooke wrote to Marsh saying that royalties from his book should go to Gibson, Abercrombie and de la Mare if he dies, Brooke put in brackets that "John is childless". Although no surname was used, this most likely referred to Drinkwater and explains why Brooke didn't include him as a beneficiary.

If Catherine Abercrombie's memory was accurate, Drinkwater and Gibson were at The Gallows when the idea for *New Numbers* was first discussed in the early summer of 1913. She was as enthusiastic as the three men, and offered to help with the administration and secretarial work. But there seem to have been some second thoughts about Drinkater's involvement. Eddie Marsh, during a visit to The Gallows in August 1913, wrote to Brooke that Abercrombie and Gibson "are rather uneasy about Drinkwater as a contributor to *New Numbers*, as they think he only means to send them what he can't get paid for by magazines! I think it would be best to chuck him." (Hassall, Marsh, p. 242) Marsh suggested Flecker or Bottomley instead. A more likely reason for concern would have been Drinkwater's busy full-time job managing the theatre.

Nothing came of the suggestion, however, and five Drinkwater poems appeared in the first *New Numbers*, including **'The Boundaries'** and **'A Town Window'**. The latter, reprinted in *Georgian Poetry 1913-1915* and *Swords and Ploughshares*, illustrates Abercrombie's comment about Drinkwater's poetry: "Commonplace things ceased to be that in his enjoyment of them: they were all part of the inexhaustibly marvellous privilege of being alive." (Abercrombie's address at Drinkwater's memorial service at the Church of St Martin in the Fields, 2 April 1937, reprinted as an introduction to vol. III of Drinkwater's *Collected Poems*.)

Drinkwater made frequent visits to The Gallows to help plan *New Numbers*. Catherine Abercrombie recalled them, especially the time "he turned up with a sleeping-bag and announced that he wanted to set up camp under the great elms at the bottom of the garden, but the first night he roused us up in great perturbation to let him in. . . . " It seems that a horse in the next field had frightened him. (Abercrombie, C., p.793) She paints an idyllic scene of Abercrombie, Gibson and Drinkwater often sitting outdoors in the evening, reading their latest poems while supper cooked in an iron pot over the fire. John Haines recalled Drinkwater at Ryton, "talking ecstatically on Poetic Drama in that enchanted garden, with a cherry orchard close by." And for miles around there were "daffodils, daffodils everywhere." (Haines, *Gloucester Journal*, 12 January 1935) **'The Broken Gate'** evokes that north Gloucestershire countryside of fruit trees and daffodils.

Drinkwater was deeply affected by Brooke's death, and wrote a poem titled **'Rupert Brooke'**. He also wrote a 22-page essay on Brooke that he had printed as a small book, at his own expense, in 1916. This was reprinted in his 1918 volume of essays called *Prose Papers*, along with an essay on Brooke's thesis about John Webster.

Drinkwater continued to write poetry in the years following the Dymock idyll. A volume of poems called *Swords and Ploughshares* was published in 1915. I've chosen **'Mamble'** because it shows Drinkwater's skills as a lyric poet and his love of ordinary countryside. One of Drinkwater's most well-known poems is **'Cotswold Love'**, another fine lyrical poem published in *Tides* in 1917. At this time Drinkwater was discovering the beauty of another part of the Cotswolds. He had become friends with the artist William Rothenstein, a painter who had bought a farmhouse at Far Oakridge, near Stroud, and was playing host there to many artists.

In 1916 Drinkwater published *Olton Pools*, which contained **'Immortality'** – a poem that mentions Dymock and, at least in the first six lines, sounds to me as if it could have been written by Brooke rather than Drinkwater. It seems likely that Brooke is the friend ("who died in his young beauty") referred to in part II. The references to seas and Dymock orchards obviously have connections with Brooke.

Another poem that mentions Dymock – and shows the lasting influence of his visits to the area – is **'Blackbird'**. It was published in *Loyalties* in 1919. But the Drinkwater poem most redolent of Dymock is **'Daffodils'**, also from *Olton Pools*. Here are references to Dymock, Ryton woods, friends who make rhymes, and daffodils that are aglow – as they still are today although not in such profusion as when the poets were there. At about this time Drinkwater moved to Far Oakridge to be near William Rothenstein and to live in this corner of what he called the "enchanted Cotswold country". Later he was involved in the early days of the Malvern Festival, which was founded by his good friend and colleague Barry Jackson in 1929.

The Boundaries

Although beyond the track of unseen stars
    Imagination strove in weariless might,
Yet loomed at last inviolable bars
    That bound my farthest flight.

And when some plain old carol in the street
    Quickened a shining angel in my brain,
I knew that even his passionate wings should beat
    Upon those bars in vain.

And then I asked if God omnipotent
    Himself was caught within the snare, or free,
And would the bars at his command relent.—
    And none could answer me.

A Town Window

Beyond my window in the night
    Is but a drab inglorious street,
Yet there the frost and clean starlight
    As over Warwick woods are sweet.

Under the grey drift of the town
    The crocus works among the mould
As eagerly as those that crown
    The Warwick spring in flame and gold.

And when the tramway down the hill
    Across the cobbles moans and rings,
There is about my window-sill
    The tumult of a thousand wings.

The Broken Gate

I know a little broken gate
    Beneath the apple-boughs and pines,
The seasons lend it coloured state,
    And round its hinge the ivy twines—
The ivy and the bloomless rose,
    And autumn berries flaming red;
The pine its gracious scent bestows,
    The apple-boughs their treasure shed.

It opens on an orchard hung
    With heavy-laden boughs that spill
Their brown and yellow fruit among
    The withered stems of daffodil:
The river from its shallows freed
    Here falls upon a stirless peace,
The tides of time suspended lead
    The tired spirit to release.

A little land of mellowed ease
    I find beyond my broken gate,
I hear amid the laden trees
    A magic song, and there elate
I pass along from sound and sight
    Of men who fret the world away,—
I gather rich and rare delight
    Where every day is holy day.

Rupert Brooke
(Died April 23, 1915)

Today I have talked with old Euripides;
    Shakespeare this morning sang for my content
Of chimney-sweepers; through the Carian trees
    Comes beating still the nightingales' lament;
The Tabard ales today are freshly brewed;
    Wordsworth is with me, mounting Loughrigg Fell;
All timeless deaths in Lycid are renewed,
    And basils blossom yet for Isabel.

Quick thoughts are these; they do not pass; they gave
    Only to death such little, casual things
As are the noteless levies of the grave,—
    Sad flesh, weak verse, and idle marketings.
So my mortality for yours complains,
While our immortal fellowship remains.

Mamble

I never went to Mamble
That lies above the Teme,
So I wonder who's in Mamble,
And whether people seem
Who breed and brew along there
As lazy as the name,
And whether any song there
Sets alehouse wits aflame.

The finger-post says Mamble,
And that is all I know
Of the narrow road to Mamble,
And should I turn and go
To that place of lazy token
That lies above the Teme,
There might be a Mamble broken
That was lissom in a dream.

So leave the road to Mamble
And take another road
To as good a place as Mamble
Be it lazy as a toad;
Who travels Worcester county
Takes any place that comes
When April tosses bounty
To the cherries and the plums.

Cotswold Love

Blue skies are over Cotswold
And April snows go by,
The lasses turn their ribbons
For April's in the sky,
And April is the season
When Sabbath girls are dressed,
From Rodboro' to Campden,
In all their silken best.

An ankle is a marvel
When first the buds are brown,
And not a lass but knows it
From Stow to Gloucester town.
And not a girl goes walking
Along the Cotswold lanes
But knows men's eyes in April
Are quicker than their brains.

It's little that it matters,
So long as you're alive,
If you're eighteen in April,
Or rising sixty-five,
When April comes to Amberley
With skies of April blue,
And Cotswold girls are briding
With slyly tilted shoe.

Immortality

I

When other beauty governs other lips,
    And snowdrops come to strange and happy springs,
When seas renewed bear yet unbuilded ships,
    And alien hearts know all familiar things,
When frosty nights bring comrades to enjoy
    Sweet hours at hearths where we no longer sit,
When Liverpool is one with dusty Troy,
    And London famed as Attica for wit . . .
How shall it be with you, and you, and you,
    How with us all who have gone greatly here
In friendship, making some delight, some true
    Song in the dark, some story against fear?
Shall song still walk with love, and life be brave,
And we, who were all these, be but the grave?

II

No; lovers yet shall tell the nightingale
    Sometimes a song that we of old time made,
And gossips gathered at the twilight ale
    Shall say, "Those two were friends," or, "Unafraid
Of bitter thought were those because they loved
    Better than most." And sometimes shall be told
How one, who died in his young beauty, moved,
    As Astrophel, those English hearts of old.
And the new seas shall take the new ships home
    Telling how yet the Dymock orchards stand,
And you shall walk with Julius at Rome,
    And Paul shall be my fellow in the Strand;
There in the midst of all those words shall be
Our names, our ghosts, our immortality.

Blackbird

He comes on chosen evenings,
My blackbird bountiful, and sings
Over the gardens of the town
Just at the hour the sun goes down.
His flight across the chimneys thick,
By some divine arithmetic,
Comes to his customary stack,
And couches there his plumage black,
And there he lifts his yellow bill,
Kindled against the sunset, till
These suburbs are like Dymock woods
Where music has her solitudes,
And while he mocks the winter's wrong
Rapt on his pinnacle of song,
Figured above our garden plots
Those are celestial chimney-pots.

Daffodils

Again, my man of Lady Street,
Your daffodils have come, the sweet
Bell daffodils that are aglow
In Ryton woods now, where they go
Who are my friends and make good rhymes.

They come, these very daffodils,
From that same flight of Gloucester hills,
Where Dymock dames and Dymock men
Have cider kegs and flocks in pen,
For I've been there a thousand times.

Your petals are enchanted still
And when those tongues of Orphic skill
Bestowed upon that Ryton earth
A benediction for your birth,
Sun-daffodils that now I greet.

Because, brave daffodils, you bring
Colour and savour of a spring
That Ryton blood is quick to tell,
You should be borne, if all were well,
In golden carts to Lady Street.

RUPERT BROOKE
(1887-1915)

Most people think of Brooke as a war poet, despite the fact that only a small percentage of his poetic output occurred after the outbreak of war. Pedants might argue that Brooke wasn't really a 'Dymock Poet'. They could point out that he visited the area on only two occasions (unless other visits went unrecorded and biographers have found no evidence of them). Both visits were brief. And there isn't any one poem that was written while he was in the area or has any theme deriving specifically from it. On the other hand 'The Soldier', one of the most famous sonnets in the English language, appeared in *New Numbers*, which was edited by Abercrombie and Gibson and posted to subscribers from Dymock. In fact, it was Gibson who decided to change the name of 'The Recruit' to 'The Soldier.' It might even be claimed that without Gibson and Abercrombie asking Brooke to write some poems for the final issue of *New Numbers*, there might never have been any war poems from Brooke.

Brooke's initial link with the Dymock Poets was through Eddie Marsh, whose moral and financial support was crucial for many young artists rebelling against the Victorian and Edwardian eras. Marsh not only edited *Georgian Poetry*, but is also credited with successfully marketing it (in today's terminology). "Marsh took the first significant step toward making modern poetry popular," concluded Ross (p.108). Marsh's money underpinned the publication of *Georgian Poetry*, and later of *New Numbers*. Marsh doted on Brooke; as a result there were introductions to politicians and actresses as well as artists and writers. Through Marsh's generosity Brooke had a base in London - a room in Marsh's spacious flat at Gray's Inn. Brooke's first meeting with Drinkwater was during lunch at the flat in September 1912, arranged to discuss the possible publication of works by the new 'Georgian' poets. Gibson was there too, having met Brooke for the first time a few days earlier. When Marsh visited Dymock to see Abercrombie and Gibson in 1913 and 1914, he sent long letters to Brooke (who was abroad for a year) about how he spent his time and what the two poets were writing. Marsh also served as a post office while Brooke was away, forwarding poems for *New Numbers* to the editorial office at The Gallows.

Brooke, often accompanied by Marsh, saw several of the Dymock Poets in London. Brooke was occasionally at the St George's restaurant (where Thomas first met Frost), or reading poems at the Poetry Bookshop, and there were meals with Eddie Marsh to which Gibson, Drinkwater and others were invited. Gibson attended Brooke's farewell party on 20 May 1913 before he set sail for America. When Brooke returned a year later from his travels in North America and the South Seas, a party was arranged for Thursday June 11, 1914, which Gibson attended. The next evening Abercrombie dined with Brooke and Marsh at Simpsons, along with some Americans Brooke had met in Chicago. This was the first time Brooke and Abercrombie met. The next night, joined by Gibson and Monro, they all went to the ballet and talked late into the night. (Turner, p.136f)

Thomas and Brooke visited each other (in Steep and Cambridge) in 1910, although Brooke went to Steep with a dual purpose. He was in love with Noel Olivier, a pupil at the nearby Bedales school, and arranged to see her at the same time that he was visiting Thomas. Thomas reviewed Brooke's *Poems 1911* in the *Daily Chronicle* and forecast that Brooke would be a great poet. "Copies should be bought by every one over forty who has never been under forty. It will be a revelation," he told readers. (Turner, p.88) In May 1913 Brooke wrote to apologise for not coming to see Thomas before leaving for America: "I sail next Thursday. I shall stay – I don't know how long. Perhaps next March's primroses'll fetch me back." Brooke asked if Thomas would be in London early next week. "If so you might charge me with some message for the continent of America. . . and I could leave the muses of England in your keeping – I do that anyhow." (Brooke, p.459)

Brooke had strong attachments to people throughout his life whom he did not see as much as he would have wished. The main evidence of his attachment to Abercrombie and Gibson is his instructions to his mother and to Marsh to make them recipients of his royalties, his capital allowance and the inheritance he would have had from her. A month before his death, Brooke wrote to Marsh: "I've tried to arrange that some money should go to Wilfrid & Lascelles & de la Mare to help them write good stuff, instead of me." (Keynes, p.669) When one considers the wide range of friends Brooke had – through Cambridge, Bloomsbury, the Fabian Society and Eddie Marsh among others – his concern to ensure that Gibson and Abercrombie were beneficiaries is more significant than time spent – or not spent – in Dymock.

The first poem below is the only one in this selection that was not published in *New Numbers*. It is 'The Way that Lovers Use', dated 1913 in the *Collected Poems* and first published in Harold Monro's *Poetry and Drama* for December 1913. Frost sent a copy of the magazine to his American friend John Bartlett, containing marginal notes he had made on almost all the poems. Most of his remarks were several sentences long, but next to 'The Way that Lovers Use' was one word: "Wow!" (Anderson, p.75)

Brooke was delighted when Gibson asked him to be the fourth contributor to a magazine that he and Abercrombie were planning to produce at The

Gallows. At first it was to be called *New Shilling Garland* and then *Gallows Garland*, after a series of books edited by Laurence Binyon. When Gibson wrote about the idea to Brooke, then in Canada, he said "You are, of course, too young to remember *The Shilling Garland*." From Toronto in July 1913 Brooke replied to Gibson: "I think the G.G. is a great idea. I'm all for amalgamating our four publics, the more that mine is far the smallest! I'm afraid I shall be outwritten by you fluent giants. . . . I'm very much pleased and excited about the scheme, and I'll 'come in', right in, without knocking...." (Brooke, p.486)

But not before sending Gibson an imaginary Table of Contents, which is a witty parody of their respective styles:

1. Lascelles Abercrombie: Haman and Mordecai, pp.1-178*
2. John Drinkwater: The Sonority of God: An Ode, pp.79-143
3. W.W. Gibson: Poor Bloody Bill: A Tale, pp.144-187
4. Rupert Brooke: Oh, Dear! Oh, Dear! A Sonnet, p.188
5. Lascelles Abercrombie: Asshur-Bani-Pal and Og, pp.189-254
6. John Drinkwater: William Morris: An Appreciation in Verse, pp.255-377
7. W. W. Gibson: Gas-Stoves: No. 1. A Brave Poor Thing, pp.377-594

Once again the name was changed – this time to *New Numbers* – and Brooke wrote to Eddie Marsh on September 6, 1913 that "I think it's silly changing it from Gallows Garland." (Brooke, p.506) But this didn't stop him from sending some poems, including '**Sonnet (Suggested by some of the Proceedings of the Society for Psychical Research)**'. Here we see Brooke exploring the possibility of perfect love, which can take place when we have physically died – then there will be "pure converse" as we "learn all we lacked before." When *The Times* gave a glowing review to *New Numbers*, it quoted from this poem. For Christopher Hassall, this and the war sonnets 4 and 5 (see below) are among the best sonnets in the English language (Hassall, Brooke, p. 531)

The only poem by Brooke in *New Numbers 2* was '**Heaven**', in which he made use of Plato's concept of universal ideas or forms while at the same time writing a witty satire on Victorian religion. He had sent it to Marsh from New Zealand and Marsh took it to The Old Nailshop when he visited the Gibsons in February 1914. The Gibsons had only been married for two months, and Marsh was keen to see how they were settling into their rural retreat. He wrote back to Brooke: "I'm enraptured by the fish's heaven, it is brilliantly amusing, and also beautiful. It certainly mustn't come out in *New Numbers* as

*Brooke probably wrote 'pp.1-78' but this is how it appears in Keynes' edition.

all the clergyman would at once withdraw their subscriptions!" Of his weekend with the Gibsons he wrote: ". . . their cottage is very nice, all with a perfect sense of style – he couldn't possibly have done better for himself. . . . We had a lovely walk, it's beautiful country. . . . " (Hassall, Marsh, p.268)

That summer, when Brooke was back in England, he arranged for Gibson to send the second issue of *New Numbers* to his American friend, Russell Loines, to whom Brooke himself wrote that "The thing is going pretty well: about seven or eight hundred of each number, which pays expenses very easily, and leaves a good bit for division. It goes on selling steadily, & I suppose it always will. . . I hope so, for the more it's sold, the more poetry, & less reviews, Abercrombie & Gibson can write: & the better for the world." (Brooke, p.597)

Brooke returned from the South Seas via Chicago and New York, arriving in London on June 6, 1914. He spent the next few weeks "seeing old friends and making new ones – including Lascelles Abercrombie, whom he met for the first time, though they had long been friends by proxy and by correspondence." (Marsh, Memoir, p. 121). Gibson went to London for the "welcome home" party. He and Brooke were especially fond of each other, and Brooke affectionately called him Wibson – perhaps because Gibson often signed himself W. W. Gibson. In a letter from Fiji to Jacques Raverat, Brooke had planned a walking tour "on the Poet's Round," starting from Charing Cross and stopping to see de la Mare at Anerley, Davies at Sevenoaks, Belloc at Kingsland, "then up to Wibson on the borders of Gloucestershire," and returning via the Chilterns "where Masefield and Chesterton dwell." (Brooke, p.539)

The walking tour never took place, but Brooke went to Gloucestershire in July 1914 to see Abercrombie and Gibson about the third issue of *New Numbers*. They had probably received most of Brooke's poems by now, as Marsh had been forwarding them after receiving them from Brooke. "Fire the verse on to Wilfrid" he wrote to Marsh from the Hotel Lorina, in Papeete, Tahiti on March 7 1914. (Brooke, p.565) While living in Mataiea, a native village about 30 miles from Papeete, he wrote '**Retrospect**', one of the five Brooke poems printed in *New Numbers 3*. While in the South Seas, Brooke had Robert Louis Stevenson much on his mind, and the poem reflects this (see Read, p. 216). Hassall sees it as an elegy to the memory of Ka Cox, after their complex relationship had ended. Sending more poems to Eddie Marsh from Samoa, he says: "These go to Wilfrid immediately. A few more are half out & shall follow somewhen. I am becoming indistinguishable from R.L.S., both in thinness, in literary style, & in dissociation from England." (Brooke, p. 524) A couple of weeks later, writing to Edmund Gosse, he describes his protective feelings towards the natives and concludes: "And that perhaps is what Stevenson felt. I don't know enough about him. His memory is sweet there, in Samoa; especially among the natives." (Brooke, p. 531) He goes on to describe his visit to Stevenson's grave on a steep hill above Vailima – "It's a high and lovely spot." (Within 18 months Brooke too would be buried on a high and lovely spot, but on an island in the Aegean.)

Hassall concluded that these three poems – 'Sonnet', 'Heaven' and 'Retrospect' – plus a few others, "are the poems which best reflect Brooke's character." (Hassall, Brooke, p. 434)

Three poems from the last issue of *New Numbers* are included here. 'The Treasure' was presumably written in August 1914, at a time when he was increasingly concerned about the war and whether he should try to get to the front as soon as possible. The poem was sent to Marsh from Rugby on 24 August; there was no other text, just the poem headed "*Unpacking* or *Contemplation* or *The Store*". But it was printed in the final issue of *New Numbers* as 'The Treasure'. There are some minor differences in punctuation between the two versions, and the fourth line of the second stanza originally was "Of song & sky & flower & face;". (Brooke, p.612)

The memories he had stored up and hoped to unpack one day might well have been of his time at The Gallows a few weeks earlier. In the letter to Loines mentioned above he says "I've stayed two days with Gibson. . . . Abercrombie's [cottage] is the most beautiful you can imagine: black-beamed & rose-covered. And a porch where one drinks great mugs of cider, & looks at fields of poppies in the corn. A life that makes London a very foolish affair. . . . There's some good stuff of Wilfrid Gibson's in next *New Numbers*. I doubt if there's any other news of *first-rate* importance." (Brooke, p.598) He was to recall those poppies when he visited The Gallows for the last time at the end of January 1915, when the Frosts as well as the Abercrombies were living there. Before leaving he gazed at the field that had been ablaze with poppies the previous summer, turned to Catherine Abercrombie and said "I shall always remember that – always." (Abercrombie, C.)

The selection ends with two poems from the famous sonnet sequence that Brooke wrote in December 1914 while preparing, with the Hood Regiment, to take part in the Dardanelles campaign. He finished them at Rugby, where he went to spend Christmas with his mother. Gibson and Abercrombie agreed to delay the publication of *New Numbers 4* as Brooke was still working on the sonnets. He posted them to Abercrombie at The Gallows in January, and proofs reached him at camp near Blandford in Dorset. "These proofs have come," he wrote to Eddie Marsh on January 24. "God, they're in the rough, these five camp-children – 4 and 5 are good enough, and there are phrases in the rest." (Marsh, Memoir, p. 134) In a letter to Drinkwater later in the month he wrote: "Come and die. It'll be great fun. And there's great health in the preparation. The theatre's no place, now. If you stay there you'll not be able to start afresh with us all when we come back. . . . But first, or anyhow, borrow a car, pick up Wilfrid and Lascelles on Saturday, and come to Dorset; and on Saturday afternoon, or Sunday, or both, walk over the Roman downs with me, and drink greatly, and talk once more. . . . " (Brooke, p.655)

I have chosen 'The Dead', number four in the sonnet sequence, because Brooke liked it (see above), but also for personal preference and because it is more pastoral than the others. The final poem in this selection, 'The Soldier', needs no introduction. The sudden popularity of this poem, combined with the mythologizing of Brooke, produced an inevitable reaction later and it became fashionable to deride the patriotic sentiments the poem expresses. But critics forget that Wilfred Owen and Siegfried Sassoon had, early in the war, expressed sentiments similar to those in Brooke's war sonnets. It is helpful to bear in mind that Brooke had been on active service at Antwerp and wrote to a friend on November 11, 1914:

"It hurts me, this war. Because I was fond of Germany. There are such good things in her, and I'd always hoped she'd get away from Prussia and the oligarchy in time. If it had been a mere war between us and them I'd have hated fighting. But I'm glad to be doing it for Belgium. That's what breaks the heart to see and hear of. I marched through Antwerp, deserted, shelled, and burning, one night, and saw ruined houses, dead men and horses: railway-trains with their lines taken up and twisted and flung down as if a child had been playing with a toy. And the whole heaven and earth was lit up by the glare from the great lakes and rivers of burning petrol, hills and spires of flame. That was like Hell, a Dantesque Hell, terrible." (Brooke, p.632)

When Brooke sent Gibson a copy of the poem it was titled 'The Recruit'. Gibson thought that 'The Soldier' would be better, and that is how it has always appeared. There is no published evidence as to whether this was discussed with Brooke.

While the poem made Brooke famous, it also drew attention to *New Numbers* and put Dymock on the literary map of England. Marsh sent Brooke, aboard his troopship, a glowing review of *New Numbers 4* from the *Times Literary Supplement*, which singled out Brooke's war sonnets for their selfless patriotism. He also sent a clipping from *The Times* reporting that on April 5 (Easter Sunday) Dean Inge had read 'The Soldier' from the pulpit of St Paul's and then remarked that Brooke would rank "with our great poets;" however, while admiring Brooke's patriotism the Dean also criticised the absence of

Christian sentiment in the poem. When his friend Denis Browne visited his cabin to say he had seen the article from *The Times*, a very ill Brooke could only mumble that he was sorry Dean Inge did not think him quite as good as Isaiah. (Hassall, Brooke, p. 507).

These were almost the last words he spoke. He died two days later, on April 23, and is buried on the Greek island of Skyros. In a letter to Robert Frost in May 1915, Thomas said that he was re-reading Rupert Brooke and writing an article about him: "You heard perhaps that he died on April 23rd of sunstroke on the way to the Dardanelles? All the papers are full of his 'beauty' and of an eloquent last sonnet beginning 'If I should die'. He was eloquent. Men never spoke ill of him." (Thomas, Thomas, p.109)

The Way That Lovers Use

The way that lovers use is this;
They bow, catch hands, with never a word,
And their lips meet, and they do kiss,
—So I have heard.

They queerly find some healing so,
And strange attainment in the touch;
There is a secret lovers know,
I have read as much.

And theirs no longer joy nor smart,
Changing or ending, night or day;
But mouth to mouth, and heart on heart,
—So lovers say.

Sonnet *(Suggested by some of the Proceedings of the Society for Psychical Research)*

Not with vain tears, when we're beyond the sun,
We'll beat on the substantial doors, nor tread
Those dusty high-roads of the aimless dead
Plaintive for earth; but rather turn and run
Down some close-covered by-way of the air,
Some low sweet alley between wind and wind,
Stoop under faint gleams, thread the shadows, find
Some whispering ghost-forgotten nook, and there

Spend in pure converse our eternal day;
Think each in each, immediately wise;
Learn all we lacked before; hear, know and say
What this tumultuous body now denies;
And feel, who have laid our groping hands away;
And see, no longer blinded by our eyes.

1913

Heaven

Fish (fly-replete, in depth of June,
Dawdling away their wat'ry noon)
Ponder deep wisdom, dark or clear,
Each secret fishy hope or fear.
Fish say, they have their Stream and Pond;
But is there anything Beyond?
This life cannot be All, they swear,
For how unpleasant, if it were!
One may not doubt that, somehow, Good
Shall come of Water and of Mud;
And, sure, the reverent eye must see
A Purpose in Liquidity.
We darkly know, by Faith we cry,
The future is not Wholly Dry.
Mud unto mud!—Death eddies near—
Not here the appointed End, not here!
But somewhere, beyond Space and Time,
Is wetter water, slimier slime!
And there (they trust) there swimmeth One
Who swam ere rivers were begun,
Immense, of fishy form and mind,
Squamous, omnipotent, and kind;
And under that Almighty Fin,
The littlest fish may enter in.
Oh! never fly conceals a hook,
Fish say, in the Eternal Brook,
But more than mundane weeds are there,
And mud, celestially fair;
Fat caterpillars drift around,
And Paradisal grubs are found;
Unfading moths, immortal flies,
And the worm that never dies.
And in that Heaven of all their wish,
There shall be no more land, say fish.

Retrospect

In your arms was still delight,
Quiet as a street at night;
And thoughts of you, I do remember,
Were green leaves in a darkened chamber,
Were dark clouds in a moonless sky.
Love, in you, went passing by,
Penetrative, remote, and rare,
Like a bird in the wide air,
And, as the bird, it left no trace
In the heaven of your face.
In your stupidity I found
The sweet hush after a sweet sound.
All about you was the light
That dims the greying end of night;
Desire was the unrisen sun,
Joy the day not yet begun,
With tree whispering to tree,
Without wind, quietly.
Wisdom slept within your hair,
And Long-Suffering was there,
And, in the flowing of your dress,
Undiscerning tenderness.
And when you thought, it seemed to me,
Infinitely, and like a sea,
About the slight world you had known
Your vast unconsciousness was thrown. . . .
        O haven without wave or tide!
Silence, in which all songs have died!
Holy book, where hearts are still!
And home at length under the hill!
O mother-quiet, breasts of peace,
        Where love itself would faint and cease
O infinite deep I never knew,
I would come back, come back to you,
Find you, as a pool unstirred,
Kneel down by you, and never a word,
Lay my head, and nothing said,
In your hands, ungarlanded;
And a long watch you would keep;
And I should sleep, and I should sleep!

Mataiea, January 1914

The Treasure

When colour goes home into the eyes,
And lights that shine are shut again,
With dancing girls and sweet birds' cries
Behind the gateways of the brain;
And that no-place which gave them birth, shall close
The rainbow and the rose:—

Still may Time hold some golden space
Where I'll unpack that scented store
Of song and flower and sky and face,
And count, and touch, and turn them o'er,
Musing upon them; as a mother, who
Has watched her children all the rich day through,
Sits, quiet-handed, in the fading light,
When children sleep, ere night.

August 1914

IV. The Dead

These hearts were woven of human joys and cares,
Washed marvellously with sorrow, swift to mirth.
The years had given them kindness. Dawn was theirs,
And sunset, and the colours of earth.
These had seen movement, and heard music; known
Slumber and waking; loved; gone proudly friended;
Felt the quick stir of wonder; sat alone;
Touched flowers and furs and cheeks. All this is ended.

There are waters blown by changing winds to laughter
And lit by the rich skies, all day. And after,
Frost, with a gesture, stays the waves that dance
And wandering loveliness. He leaves a white
Unbroken glory, a gathered radiance,
A width, a shining peace, under the night.

V. The Soldier

If I should die, think only this of me:
  That there's some corner of a foreign field
That is for ever England. There shall be
  In that rich earth a richer dust concealed;
A dust whom England bore, shaped, made aware,
  Gave, once, her flowers to love, her ways to roam,
A body of England's, breathing English air,
  Washed by the rivers, blest by suns of home.

And think, this heart, all evil shed away,
  A pulse in the eternal mind, no less
    Gives somewhere back the thoughts by England given;
Her sights and sounds; dreams happy as her day;
  And laughter, learnt of friends; and gentleness,
    In hearts at peace, under an English heaven.

ROBERT FROST
(1874-1963)

Robert Frost was 38 when he left New England for a long visit to England. He had worked as a farmer and teacher in Massachusetts and New Hampshire, but had always wanted to be a poet. Only a few of his poems had been published in American newspapers and magazines; and in England he was completely unknown as a poet. When he arrived in London in 1912 he had with him a trunk full of unpublished poems in various stages of completion. His first book, *A Boy's Will*, was published in London in 1913 by David Nutt, one of the oldest and most respected publishing firms in London at that time (Walsh, p.38). Reviews were encouraging but not overly enthusiastic. Still, Frost's publisher felt confident enough to bring out another volume of his the following year. This time there was widespread acclaim for *North of Boston*, and Frost soon had a reputation as an important new poet on both sides of the Atlantic. By the time of his death in 1963 his reputation extended around the world; he was a cultural ambassador for America, a poet laureate to the world.

Frost, his wife, and four young children stayed at a London hotel for a week, while he went looking for long-term accommodation. He found a bungalow in Beaconsfield, near the new railway to London, and surrounded by Chiltern beechwoods. Two of his visits to London were especially important – when he brought his manuscript to a publisher, and when he attended the opening party for the Poetry Bookshop. At the Poetry Bookshop he met many of the Georgian poets, including Gibson and Abercrombie. They admired his first book of poems, and when Gibson was planning to move to Gloucestershire at the end of 1913, they suggested that he should leave Beaconsfield to join them in real countryside. He did this early in 1914, living first at Little Iddens, and then at The Gallows.

Unravelling when and where Frost's early poems were written is not always easy. This is especially true because he seemed to enjoy, later in life, playfully confusing his many biographers and interviewers. John W. Haines, a Gloucester lawyer who was a close friend during Frost's Dymock days and corresponded with him later, claims that most of *Mountain Interval* (Frost's third volume, published on his return to America) was written in Gloucestershire, at Little Iddens and The Gallows. But the Mertins, who interviewed him for a bibliography they produced in 1947, wrote that ". . . the product of Frost's poetry during the Dymock interval just about matched the produce of the Little Iddens farm. It wasn't much. 'Here I wrote some poems,' he has put it; but not all of them are traceable". (Mertins, p. 25) However, recalling his time in Dymock (in the introduction he wrote to *The Masque of Reason* in 1948), Frost says that in addition to discussing poetry, and botanising with Haines and Thomas, he spent time in the Little Iddens apple orchard where he liked to sit and write.

It is likely that 'The Cow in Apple Time' was inspired by a pastoral scene in the Dymock countryside in 1914. I say this despite the fact that Frost told a biographer in the 1950s that he wrote it "after the bronze animals on the Albert Memorial." (Sergeant, p.146) I cannot find any such animals on the Albert Memorial, and have been told by experts that there have never been animals – bronze or otherwise – on it at any time. So perhaps Frost's memory was faulty. He did spend a week in London early in 1914, before moving to Gloucestershire, taking the family around some of the places that tourists visited, so it is likely that he visited the Albert Memorial at that time. And he must have worked on the poem while living at Little Iddens in 1914 as it was published in Harold Monro's December 1914 issue of *Poetry and Drama*. Three other Frost poems were published in this same issue – 'The Smile', 'Putting in the Seed', and 'The Sound of Trees' – and Frost wrote to Monro to thank him for "placing me so well in such a good number of P & D". (Frost, p.143)

'Putting in the Seed' was written at Little Iddens, according to Sergeant (p.127). But the subject matter both here and in 'To Earthward' is universal – love between man and woman, and love of the earth. Eleanor Farjeon has left us a vivid picture of the Frost and Thomas families digging the potato patch beside Little Iddens (Farjeon, p.89). If Frost's memory was accurate, then 'To Earthward' was also written at Little Iddens. "Frost had very rarely written poetry in the diffusion of outdoors," says Sergeant. "But it was at Little Iddens, he assures me, 'under a plum tree' that he wrote 'To Earthward'." (p.125) Writing to Bernard de Voto 24 years later Frost said: "One of the greatest changes my nature has undergone is of record in To Earthward and indeed elsewhere for the discerning. In my school days I simply could not go on and do the best I could with a copy book I had once blotted. I began life wanting perfection and determined to have it. I got so I ceased to expect it and could do without it. Now I find I actually crave the flaws in human handwork." (Frost, p.482)

'The Sound of Trees' was probably written when Frost and his family moved to Abercrombie's cottage, The Gallows, in September 1914 to save money in wartime conditions. It is one of two poems that have, as a backdrop, Abercrombie's thatched cottage near the woods at Ryton. He told Sergeant that the poem was "written for Abercrombie" and is the "only one I wrote in

England that had an English *subject*." (Sergeant, p.146) But the sound and sight of wind in the trees must have been familiar to him from all his years in New England. According to Haines, Frost said there were two influences: the elms near Abercrombie's cottage and a wood he remembered in New Hampshire (Street, p.128). The trees seemed to be speaking to him about difficult decisions that had to be made as a result of the war. In 1916 Gibson wrote to Frost, who was now back in America: "*Your* trees at the Gallows, the whole group of elms, and our elm over the shed in the field, were all blown down in the same storm in the spring." (Francis, p.182) The poem was published in *Mountain Interval*, at the very end and in italics. (The first and last poems in *A Boy's Will* were also printed in italics.)

'**The Thatch**' also has The Gallows as a backdrop. It was Frost's wife Elinor, presumably waiting with the light on inside, who had been so keen to go to England and live "under thatch". They were now doing that, but domestic quarrels and Frost's moodiness did not suddenly disappear. Frost (like Edward Thomas) was prone to deep if temporary depressions, after which he felt guilty at the anguish he caused his wife when these moods descended upon him. The poem was originally published in Frost's *West-Running Brook* (1928) with a note dating it to 1914.

If that is so, Frost left 'The Thatch' out of the reckoning when writing to the American, Amy Lowell, to correct some biographical errors about him in her 1917 book, *Tendencies in Modern American Poetry*. He was concerned at her implication that Gibson and Abercrombie had influenced his poetry, and he asked her to note "that I didn't meet Gibson till I was putting the last touches on North of Boston and I didn't meet Abercrombie till after the MS was in David Nutt's hands. It was the book that got me invited down to live with those fellows in the country. I had begun writing it in 1905. I wrote the bulk of it in 1913. . . . You see if any of my work was in danger of Gibsonian or Abercrombian influence it was what I wrote of Mountain Interval in 1914: Birches and The Hill Wife and Putting in the Seed and The Sound of Trees. None of this greatly matters, but since you seem bent on accuracy, you might make a marginal note of it." (Frost, p.219f)

Throughout their time in England the Frost children published a little magazine called *The Bouquet*. Their parents and friends were asked to help with contributions and drawings, and the Thomas family was soon involved with the project (see Francis – as Frost's grand-daughter, with access to her mother's papers, she has written the fullest account of this youthful creative venture). Frost's first contribution, 'Pea-sticks', appeared in the July 1914 issue of *The Bouquet* and was later published in *Mountain Interval* as '**Pea Brush**'. Frost wrote in a pocket notebook that he kept while in England: "Hollis said I could have all the brushwood I wanted to brush my peas." (Walsh, p.224) Another Frost poem, 'Locked Out', appeared in the September issue of the children's magazine. When Frost included it in the 1930 edition of *Mountain Interval*, he added the words 'As told to a child' beneath the poem's title.

'The Road Not Taken' is one of Frost's most famous poems. Yet only a tiny minority of those who read and re-read it know that it is a poem about Edward Thomas. The close friendship between Frost and Thomas is one of the most compelling aspects of the Dymock story (see Hart, Francis pp.105-06, Walsh pp.180-85 and Street pp.80-83, 103-05). According to Walsh (p.211) the poem was drafted at The Gallows towards the end of 1914, though it was altered before its publication in America where it appeared in *The Atlantic Monthly* magazine, in August 1915. It then appeared as the first poem in Frost's third book, *Mountain Interval*, published in America in 1916.

Frost maintained that the poem "was never intended as a serious effort" but was rather "a mild satire on the chronic vacillating habits of Edward Thomas" (Walsh, p.211). Because of the confusion this poem has caused, and because it illustrates the importance of irony in understanding much of Frost's work, his official biographer Lawrance Thompson wrote at length about 'The Road Not Taken' in his introduction to Frost's *Selected Letters*.

"The inspiration for it came from Frost's amusement over a familiar mannerism of his closest friend in England, Edward Thomas. While living in Gloucestershire in 1914, Frost frequently took long walks with Thomas through the countryside. Repeatedly Thomas would choose a route which might enable him to show his American friend a rare plant or vista; but it often happened that before the end of such a walk Thomas would regret the choice he had made and would sigh over what he might have shown Frost if they had taken a 'better' direction." (p.xiv)

Thompson explains that looking back and regretting previous choices was not Frost's way to approach life, and he teased Thomas about having such regrets. Back in America Frost put the final touches on the poem and sent it to Thomas without comment, "yet with the expectation that his friend would notice how the poem pivots ironically on the un-Frostian phrase, 'I shall be telling this with a sigh'. As it turned out, Frost's expectations were disappointed. Thomas missed the gentle jest because the irony had been handled too slyly, too subtly." (Thompson, p.xv)

Thomas's letter to Frost, after receiving the poem in April 1915, made it clear that he failed to see either Frost's irony or himself as the subject of the poem. Frost wrote again, and in June Thomas apologised for his mistake but seemed also to insist that the poem, which he discussed with his wife Helen, worked at another level: "I read 'The Road Not Taken' to Helen just now & she liked it entirely, & agreed with me how naturally symbolical it was." (Walsh, p.264)

When Frost read the poem to an academic audience in Boston in May 1915, something similar happened, as Frost reported to Thomas in a letter: "I suppose my little jest in the poem is too much between me and myself. I read it aloud. . . at Tufts College and while I did my best to make it obvious by my manner that I was fooling, I doubt if it wasn't taken pretty seriously. Mea culpa." (Walsh, p. 213)

But Elizabeth Sergeant says that ". . . the poem's last lines and indeed all its substance have, as I see it, a subterranean connection with his experience on that Plymouth wood road, and with the inner compulsion that in 1912 at the age of 38 sent him forth to try a new fortune on strange shores." The 'Plymouth wood road' refers to a letter Frost wrote in February 1912, just before making the difficult decision to move to England. In the letter he describes "two lonely cross-roads" that he had walked several times; "neither is much travelled" so Frost was surprised to see a man looking "all the world like myself" approaching him "to the point where our paths must intersect". (Sergeant p.87) Readers of Edward Thomas's poetry will recognize the similarity between this experience of Frost's and what Thomas describes in 'The Other'. It seems inconceivable that the two never discussed this notion of seeing someone like yourself approaching you.

I have concluded this selection with two more poems evoking the close friendship that developed between Frost and Thomas. 'Iris by Night' describes a rainbow or moonbow that seemed to encircle them both at the end of a long day's walk in August 1914. The implication is that just as these two were chosen to experience such an unusual sight, they were also divinely chosen to be the closest of friends. Describing the walk in his pocket notebook, Thomas also wrote of the strange light, heat and moisture. From Leddington they walked to Bromsberrow Heath, then via Hollybush to Castlemorton Common, then to the reservoir and British Camp on the Malverns before descending through Eastnor Park on the Ridgeway, and then back to Leddington. The poem was probably written shortly after Thomas was killed in France in 1917, but was not published until 1936.

There are two other poems Frost wrote about Thomas and the war. One is 'A Soldier', with its powerful image of Thomas as a fallen lance whose spirit nevertheless moves onward. At the end of 1916 Frost was increasingly distressed about the war: "What becomes of my hopes of three months ago when the drive on the Somme began? Something has gone wrong," he wrote to Thomas on December 7, 1916. On the back of the letter Frost wrote out a poem then titled 'France, France' but later titled '**Suggested by Talk of Peace at This Time**'. "Silly fools are full of peace talk over here.... I wrote some lines I've copied on the other side of this about the way I am struck. When I get to writing in this vein you may know I am sick or sad or something." Thomas replied, on December 31, 1916, that "I like the poem very much, because it betrays exactly what you *would* say and what you feel about saying that much. It expresses just those hesitations you or I would have at asking others to act as we think it is their cue to act." (Thomas, Letters, pp.134-5,184-5)

Frost was devastated when he received news of Thomas's death. In his letter to Helen Thomas he wrote: "He was the bravest and best and dearest man you and I have ever known. I knew from the moment when I first met him at his unhappiest that he would some day clear his mind and save his life. I have had four wonderful years with him. . . . I want to see him to tell him something. I want to tell him, what I think he liked to hear from me, that he was a poet. . . . I had meant to talk endlessly with him still, either here in our mountains as we had said or, as I found my longing was more and more, there at Leddington where we first talked of war." (Frost, p.216)

A poem emerged from Frost's grief, titled 'To Edward Thomas', but later appearing as '**To E.T.**' It was first published in *The Yale Review* in April 1920. He hesitated about publishing it, and wrote to a colleague in July 1919 to explain why: "Edward Thomas was the closest friend I ever had and I was the closest friend he ever had; and this was something I didn't wait to realize after he had died. It makes his death almost too much to talk about in The Yale Review. . . even at two years distance." (Sergeant, p.209)

The Cow in Apple Time

Something inspires the only cow of late
To make no more of a wall than an open gate,
And think no more of wall-builders than fools.
Her face is flecked with pomace and she drools
A cider syrup. Having tasted fruit,
She scorns a pasture withering to the root.
She runs from tree to tree where lie and sweeten
The windfalls spiked with stubble and worm-eaten.
She leaves them bitten when she has to fly.
She bellows on a knoll against the sky.
Her udder shrivels and the milk goes dry.

Putting in the Seed

You come to fetch me from my work tonight
When supper's on the table, and we'll see
If I can leave off burying the white
Soft petals fallen from the apple tree
(Soft petals, yes, but not so barren quite,
Mingled with these, smooth bean and wrinkled pea),
And go along with you ere you lose sight
Of what you came for and become like me,
Slave to a springtime passion for the earth.
How Love burns through the Putting in the Seed
On through the watching for that early birth
When, just as the soil tarnishes with weed,
The sturdy seedling with arched body comes
Shouldering its way and shedding the earth crumbs.

To Earthward

Love at the lips was touch
As sweet as I could bear;
And once that seemed too much;
I lived on air

That crossed me from sweet things,
The flow of – was it musk
From hidden grapevine springs
Downhill at dusk?

I had the swirl and ache
From sprays of honeysuckle
That when they're gathered shake
Dew on the knuckle.

I craved strong sweets, but those
Seemed strong when I was young;
The petal of the rose
It was that stung.

Now no joy but lacks salt
That is not dashed with pain
And weariness and fault;
I crave the stain

Of tears, the aftermark
Of almost too much love,
The sweet of bitter bark
And burning clove.

When stiff and sore and scarred
I take away my hand
From leaning on it hard
In grass and sand,

The hurt is not enough:
I long for weight and strength
To feel the earth as rough
To all my length.

The Sound of Trees

I wonder about the trees.
Why do we wish to bear
Forever the noise of these
More than another noise
So close to our dwelling place?
We suffer them by the day
Till we lose all measure of pace,
And fixity in our joys,
And acquire a listening air.
They are that that talks of going
But never gets away;
And that talks no less for knowing,
As it grows wiser and older,
That now it means to stay.
My feet tug at the floor
And my head sways to my shoulder
Sometimes when I watch trees sway,
From the window or the door.
I shall set forth for somewhere,
I shall make the reckless choice
Some day when they are in voice
And tossing so as to scare
The white clouds over them on.
I shall have less to say,
But I shall be gone.

The Thatch

Out alone in the winter rain,
Intent on giving and taking pain.
But never was I far out of sight
Of a certain upper-window light.
The light was what it was all about:
I would not go in till the light went out;
It would not go out till I came in.
Well, we should see which one would win,
We should see which one would be first to yield.
The world was a black invisible field.
The rain by rights was snow for cold.
The wind was another layer of mold.
But the strangest thing: in the thick old thatch,
Where summer birds had been given hatch,
Had fed in chorus, and lived to fledge,
Some still were living in hermitage.
And as I passed along the eaves,
So low I brushed the straw with my sleeves,
I flushed birds out of hole after hole,
Into the darkness. It grieved my soul,
It started a grief within a grief,
To think their case was beyond relief—
They could not go flying about in search
Of their nest again, nor find a perch.
They must brood where they fell in mulch and mire,
Trusting feathers and inward fire
Till daylight made it safe for a flyer.
My greater grief was by so much reduced
As I thought of them without nest or roost.
That was how that grief started to melt.
They tell me the cottage where we dwelt,
Its wind-torn thatch goes now unmended;
Its life of hundreds of years has ended
By letting the rain I knew outdoors
In on to the upper chamber floors.

Pea Brush

I walked down alone Sunday after church
     To the place where John has been cutting trees
To see for myself about the birch
     He said I could have to bush my peas.

The sun in the new-cut narrow gap
     Was hot enough for the first of May,
And stifling hot with the odor of sap
     From stumps still bleeding their life away.

The frogs that were peeping a thousand shrill
     Wherever the ground was low and wet,
The minute they heard my step went still
     To watch me and see what I came to get.

Birch boughs enough piled everywhere!—
     All fresh and sound from the recent ax.
Time someone came with cart and pair
     And got them off the wild flowers' backs.

They might be good for garden things
     To curl a little finger round,
The same as you seize cat's-cradle strings,
     And lift themselves up off the ground.

Small good to anything growing wild,
     They were crooking many a trillium
That had budded before the boughs were piled
     And since it was coming up had to come.

Locked Out

As told to a child

When we locked up the house at night,
We always locked the flowers outside
And cut them off from window light.
The time I dreamed the door was tried
And brushed with buttons upon sleeves,
The flowers were out there with the thieves.
Yet nobody molested them!
We did find one nasturtium
Upon the steps with bitten stem.
I may have been to blame for that:
I always thought it must have been
Some flower I played with as I sat
At dusk to watch the moon down early.

The Road Not Taken

Two roads diverged in a yellow wood,
And sorry I could not travel both
And be one traveler, long I stood
And looked down one as far as I could
To where it bent in the undergrowth;

Then took the other, as just as fair,
And having perhaps the better claim,
Because it was grassy and wanted wear;
Though as for that the passing there
Had worn them really about the same,

And both that morning equally lay
In leaves no step had trodden black.
Oh, I kept the first for another day!
Yet knowing how way leads on to way,
I doubted if I should ever come back.

I shall be telling this with a sigh
Somewhere ages and ages hence:
Two roads diverged in a wood, and I—
I took the one less traveled by,
And that has made all the difference.

Iris by Night

One misty evening, one another's guide,
We two were groping down a Malvern side
The last wet fields and dripping hedges home.
There came a moment of confusing lights,
Such as according to belief in Rome
Were seen of old at Memphis on the heights
Before the fragments of a former sun
Could concentrate anew and rise as one.
Light was a paste of pigment in our eyes.
And then there was a moon and then a scene
So watery as to seem submarine;
In which we two stood saturated, drowned.
The clover-mingled rowan on the ground
Had taken all the water it could as dew,
And still the air was saturated too,
Its airy pressure turned to water weight.
Then a small rainbow like a trellis gate,
A very small moon-made prismatic bow,
Stood closely over us through which to go.
And then we were vouchsafed the miracle
That never yet to other two befell
And I alone of us have lived to tell.
A wonder! Bow and rainbow as it bent,
Instead of moving with us as we went,
(To keep the pots of gold from being found)
It lifted from its dewy pediment
Its two mote-swimming many-colored ends,
And gathered them together in a ring.
And we stood in it softly circled round
From all division time or foe can bring
In a relation of elected friends.

A Soldier

He is that fallen lance that lies as hurled,
That lies unlifted now, come dew, come rust,
But still lies pointed as it plowed the dust.
If we who sight along it round the world,
See nothing worthy to have been its mark,
It is because like men we look too near,
Forgetting that as fitted to the sphere,
Our missiles always make too short an arc.
They fall, they rip the grass, they intersect
The curve of earth, and striking, break their own;
They make us cringe for metal-point on stone.
But this we know, the obstacle that checked
And tripped the body, shot the spirit on
Further than target ever showed or shone.

Suggested by Talk of Peace at This Time

France, France, I know not what is in my heart.
But God forbid that I should be more brave
As watcher from a quiet place apart
Than you are fighting in an open grave.

I will not ask more of you than you ask,
O Bravest, of yourself. But shall I less?
You know the extent of your appointed task,
Whether you still can face its bloodiness.

Not mine to say you shall not think of peace.
Not mine, not mine. I almost know your pain.
But I will not believe that you will cease,
I will not bid you cease, from being slain

And slaying till what might have been distorted
Is saved to be the Truth and Hell is thwarted.

To E.T.

I slumbered with your poems on my breast
Spread open as I dropped them half-read through
Like dove wings on a figure on a tomb
To see, if in a dream they brought of you,

I might not have the chance I missed in life
Through some delay, and call you to your face
First soldier, and then poet, and then both,
Who died a soldier-poet of your race.

I meant, you meant, that nothing should remain
Unsaid between us, brother, and this remained—
And one thing more that was not then to say:
The Victory for what it lost and gained.

You went to meet the shell's embrace of fire
On Vimy Ridge; and when you fell that day
The war seemed over more for you than me,
But now for me than you—the other way.

How over, though, for even me who knew
The foe thrust back unsafe beyond the Rhine,
If I was not to speak of it to you
And see you pleased once more with words of mine?

EDWARD THOMAS
(1878-1917)

Edward Thomas probably wrote more words in his lifetime than any of the other Dymock Poets – or so it seems from his voluminous output. But until November 1914, when he was 36 years old, he was the only Dymock Poet who had not written any poetry. One can't help wondering if he felt like the odd man out, especially when living near Frost, Gibson and Abercrombie during August 1914.

Thomas was a respected biographer and literary critic at the beginning of the century, but he always complained about the financial pressure he was under to produce a constant stream of books and articles. William Cooke estimates that between 1905 and 1915 "he wrote twenty-two books of prose and more than a million words in articles and reviews." (p.122) In a letter to Gordon Bottomley in 1903, complaining about having so much work to do, he tries to make light of it: "Inkitas inkitatum. All is ink." (Thomas, Bottomley, p.47) And in a 1911 letter to Harold Monro he wrote: "I have 3 books in hand to be done before the year's end, have written 2 short ones already this year, & have just published one & am about to correct the proofs of another." (Poetry Wales, p.48)

Thomas knew, or knew of, all the Dymock Poets before he visited Frost at Leddington for the first time in April 1914. He had reviewed poetry by both Gibson and Abercrombie, and because he was so honest in his criticism, friction occasionally resulted when he did finally meet them. In 1908 Thomas had written that "Gibson long ago swamped his small delightful gift by his abundance." (*Daily Chronicle*, May 18,1908) Four years later Thomas wrote about Gibson's *Fires, Book I*: ". . . he has been merely embellishing what would have been more effective as pieces of rough prose, extracts from a diary, or even a newspaper." (*Daily Chronicle*, 9 March 1912) Thomas knew and liked Brooke, who visited him at the Thomas home in Steep, Hampshire, a couple of times, and Thomas made a return visit to Cambridge in 1910, staying with Brooke at the Orchard in Grantchester. Thomas was one of the six judges awarding Brooke a prize for the best poem in *The Poetry Review* in 1912 (although Thomas voted for Ralph Hodgson).

Thomas's friendship with Frost makes his relationship with the other Dymock Poets pale almost into insignificance. But he was undoubtedly a welcome visitor at The Gallows. Recalling the many times he was in the area, Catherine Abercrombie said: "I think Edward was the most beautiful person I have ever seen. It was quite a shock on first meeting him unless one had been warned." (Abercrombie, C.) Elinor Frost, in June 1914, wrote to a friend: "Edward Thomas, who is a very well known critic and prose writer has been here with his two children and he is going to bring his whole family to lodge near us through August. Rob and I think everything of him. He is quite the most admirable and lovable man we have ever known." (Frost, Letters, p.126)

A great deal has been written about the remarkable similarities between Thomas and Frost, the close friendship that sprang up between them, the ideas they shared about language and poetic diction, and most of all Frost's role in Thomas's decision to start writing poetry. Within the limits of this book these matters can only be touched on, and interested readers who want to draw their own conclusions are referred to the bibliography.

It can be persuasively argued, for example, that Frost's long talks with Thomas were instrumental in the latter's beginning to write poetry at the end of 1914; but it can also be persuasively argued that other key influences were at work which made Thomas finally take the plunge. The war, for example, was important in two ways: there was no longer a market for Thomas's prose work, which gave him more time and freedom to write what he wanted; and it intensified his love of England, a subject often dealt with in his prose but arguably more suitable to poetry. Gordon Bottomley, Walter de la Mare and Eleanor Farjeon had already raised with Thomas the idea of his writing poetry – but he had rejected the suggestion. What Frost seems to have given him was confidence, at just the right time.

There is a great deal of evidence that Thomas, long before he met Frost, had been thinking about the need for a change in poetic diction. Motion claims that "from the outset, his [book] reviews had argued that the language of poetry should be colloquial." (p.60) And R. George Thomas says he "had been the champion of 'speech' and 'natural rhythm' in poetry for over a decade" before meeting Frost (Poetry Wales, p. 36). Thomas said as much to Frost, in May 1914, though in his usual self-effacing manner: "you really should start doing a book on speech and literature, or you will find me mistaking your ideas for mine and doing it myself. You can't prevent me from making use of them; I do so daily. . . . However, my [book about] 'Pater' would show you I had got on to the scent already." (Poetry Wales, p.8)

In this same letter Thomas asks "whether you can imagine me taking to verse. If you can I might get over the feeling that it is impossible – which at once obliges your good nature to say 'I can'." Frost would have had many opportunities to tell Thomas 'You can' when they walked and talked their way around Leddington and Ryton, May Hill and the Malverns, during August 1914. The Thomas family rented rooms with Mr and Mrs Chandler, who lived at Old Fields, a farmhouse just a few meadows away from the Frosts at Little Iddens. Helen Thomas recalled, many years later in *The Times*, that "They were always together and when not exploring the country they sat in the shade of a tree smoking and talking endlessly of literature and of poetry in particular." (Thomas, Thomas p.230). In fact, Thomas's three reviews of Frost's *North of Boston* in 1914 virtually set out a manifesto for contemporary poetry; to Frost it may have seemed only a matter of time until Thomas put some of these ideas into practice himself.

But Thomas didn't take to verse until the end of the year. He wrote his first five poems between 3-7 December 1914; '**March**' was one of them. He sent it with eight other poems to Frost, writing: "But I am in it and no mistake. . . . I find myself engrossed and conscious of a possible perfection as I never was in prose. . . . I have been rather pleased with some of the pieces. . . . Still, I won't begin thanking you just yet, though if you like I will put it down now that you are the only begetter right enough." (Thomas, Thomas, p.256)

In this poem Thomas certainly paid heed to what Frost told a friend that he had told Thomas: that he was already writing poetry "but in prose form where it did not declare itself and gain him recognition. I referred him to paragraphs in his book *In Pursuit of Spring* and told him to write it in verse form in exactly the same cadence." (Eckert, p.150) There are passages in the book indicating that Thomas did exactly that. The theme of 'March' recurs frequently in Thomas's poetry: how to discover nature's secret, and whether there are words adequate to express it.

'**Old Man**', the fourth poem Thomas produced, was actually written in prose form three weeks earlier – again indicating that Frost's advice was being taken seriously. Andrew Motion traces prose passages from both Thomas's autobiography and from childhood memories in *The South Country* that contain sources for the poem (p.164). When Frost sent this and several other poems by Thomas to the editor of an American poetry magazine in January 1917, he wrote: "Here I sit admiring these beautiful poems but not daring to urge them on anyone else for fear I shall be suspected of admiring them for love of their author." He concluded that "'Old Man' is the flower of the lot, isn't it?" (Frost, Letters, p.209)

Today critics often remark on how this early poem raises so many typical Thomas themes. "This sense of searching, of having mislaid the key," says Jan Marsh, "is one of the central themes of Thomas's life and work." (Marsh, p.10) And Motion notes that "'Old Man' summarises every theme and technique that Thomas used in his pursuit of wholeness." (p.168)

'**The Combe**', another early poem, has the distinction of being the first

Thomas poem to be published. Frost's talented daughter Lesley (age 14) had been producing a magazine with the help of her siblings. Although contributions were mainly by the children, 'The Combe' appeared in *The Bouquet* in April 1915. (Francis, p.121) Again, Thomas relied on prose for inspiration, this time a passage about "wooded combes" in a book review he had written of *Highways and Byways in Hampshire* (Cooke, p.53).

Thomas's best known poem is probably '**Adlestrop**', describing those few moments when the train stopped unwontedly at this station in the Cotswolds. But few people realise that the train was taking Thomas to see Robert Frost, now living in a 17th-century cottage at Leddington. 'Adlestrop' also stemmed from Thomas's prose, this time some jottings in the field notebook he always carried. In an entry for 23 June 1914 he noted the willows, the blackbirds' song and the hiss of the engine when the train stopped at Adlestrop. He also noted the willow herb and meadowsweet when, later, the train stopped near Chipping Campden. (Thomas, Poems, p.135) For details on the background and subsequent influence of this poem, see *Adlestrop Revisited* by Anne Harvey.

Thomas wrote '**Fifty Faggots**' on 13 May 1915, while doing research at the British Museum for his last book, a biography of Marlborough. This was three weeks after Rupert Brooke's death. He sent the poem to Frost, explaining in a letter that it was "founded on carrying up 50 bunts (short faggots of thin and thick brushwood mixed) and putting them against our hedge." He then asked if Frost thought the poem was "*north* of Boston only?" (Thomas, Poems, p.147) Thomas often used the title of Frost's second volume of poetry this way, says R. George Thomas, as "shorthand for poems based on rural incidents presented in simulated colloquial language." (Ibid.) By comparing the poet's future with that of the wood pile, the poem shows how the war was increasingly worrying Thomas. Two months after writing this poem, he enlisted.

In October 1914, and after a month of walking and talking with Frost in the Dymock countryside, Thomas wrote 'This England', an essay for *The Nation* about what England meant to him. In it he expressed his love for his country by describing in some detail a hot summer spent in countryside around Hereford; an unnamed friend [Frost] lived nearby and they frequently went for walks. "If talk dwindled in the traversing of a big field, the pause at gate or stile braced it again. Often we prolonged the pause whether we actually sat or not, and we talked – of flowers, childhood, Shakespeare, women, England, the war. . . " he wrote in 'This England' (Thomas, Sheaf, p.218).

Nine months later 'This England' became the basis for his poem, '**The Sun Used to Shine**'. Like the essay, it contrasts a rural idyll with the threat of war and death. Writing to Eleanor Farjeon, who was typing a fair copy of the poem from his written manuscript, Thomas said: "As to Me and Frost, I mixed up 2 forms of the 2nd verse. The 3rd sentence should be: The to be/And the late past we gave small heed." (Farjeon, p.144) Perhaps this poem should be officially retitled in future Thomas collections as 'Me and Frost'! More seriously, though, it should be read alongside Frost's 'Iris by Night' which is also about the walks they took together (see the chapter on Frost). An American professor, Jim Armstrong , has pointed out to me that the phrase "we two" appears at the beginning of both these poems.

In June 1915 Thomas had still not made up his mind whether to enlist (he was 37 years old and there was no pressure on him to do so) or to join Frost in New Hampshire. Merfyn, his teenage son, had gone to America with the Frost family in February 1915 and was still there. On 22 July, writing to tell Frost that he had decided to enlist instead, he said: "A month or two [ago] I dreamt we were walking near Leddington but we lost one another in a strange place and I woke saying to myself 'Somehow someday I shall be here again' which I made the last line of some verses." (Thomas, Poems, p.150) This was '**A Dream**' – a poem that he wrote two different versions of in June 1915. Of the 144 poems he wrote, only six are sonnets and only two of those are written in couplets; this is one of them.

Thomas wrote '**Aspens**' in July 1915 and immediately sent it to Frost, with the news that he had enlisted. Frost's sensitive reply ("You have let me follow your thought in almost every twist and turn toward this conclusion.") ends this way: "Your last poem Aspens seems the loveliest of all. You must have a volume of poetry ready for when you come marching home. I wonder if they are going to let you write to me as often as ever." (Frost, p.185)

So subtle, on first reading, is the poet's identification with the aspens that Eleanor Farjeon didn't seem to understand what he was saying. He wrote to her, after doing six hours drill: "About 'Aspens' you missed just the turn that I thought essential. *I* was the aspen. 'We' meant the trees and I with my dejected shyness. Does that clear it up, or do you think in rereading it that I have not emphasised it enough?" (Farjeon, p.153) Critics frequently compare the poem with Frost's treatment of a similar subject in 'The Sound of Trees' (see the chapter on Frost), which Thomas would have seen as it was published in *Poetry and Drama* in December 1914.

Anyone who has ever tried to write prose or poetry will appreciate the sentiments expressed in Thomas's lovely poem, '**Words**'. The original manuscript has no title, but is headed "Hucclecote – on the road from Gloucester to Coventry." (Cooke, p.248) In July 1915 Thomas visited John Haines who lived at Hucclecote, a village just outside Gloucester, before continuing on his journey north. Thomas wrote to Frost that they went "cycling about and talking of you." (Thomas, Poems, p.148) Haines also recalled the visit: "A few days before he enlisted we bicycled out to May Hill. . . and all the way he mused, and I could note him musing as he asked me questions of the scarce flowers by the way, and whilst I botanised on the hill slopes he sat on the hill. . . composing the beautiful poem 'Words', which he brought down completed for us at breakfast the next morning." (Haines)

As Cooke discusses in detail (pp.137-45), Thomas had always been interested in the nature and use of words. This can be traced, for example, in his biographies of Jefferies, Maeterlinck, Swinburne and Pater. There is space here only for one of his more amusing comments, regarding Pater: "On almost every page of his writing words are to be seen sticking out, like the raisins that will get burnt on an ill-made cake. It is clear that they have been carefully chosen as the right and effective words, but they stick out because the labour of composition has become so self-conscious and mechanical. . . . " (Ibid., p.140)

In the summer of 1915 Gordon Bottomley showed Lascelles Abercrombie and R.C. Trevelyan some copies of Thomas's poems (Bottomley was one of the few people who knew Thomas was writing poetry), as the three of them were planning *An Annual of New Poetry* for publication. Abercrombie and Trevelyan agreed at once to include them. When Thomas heard that they wanted to publish his poems, he wrote to Bottomley: "I was keeping them rather secret. However I am so pleased at having Abercrombie's liking that I should not dream of complaining." (Thomas, Bottomley, p.253)

Thomas saw the proofs of this anthology while on military leave in December 1916; eighteen of his poems were being published under the pseudonym – Edward Eastaway – that he insisted on using. The *Times Literary Supplement* reviewed the book on 29 March 1917, and John Freeman immediately sent the review to him in France. A few days before his death on April 9, he would have read these words about his poetry: "He is a real poet, with the truth in him."

But he never saw the published book, nor did he see *Poems* by Edward Eastaway published in July 1917. Thomas had given the completed manuscript for this volume to Roger Ingpen of the publishing firm of Selwyn and Blount. Ingpen was Walter de la Mare's brother-in-law, and Thomas had met him in August 1916. Eckert, Thomas's first biographer, says that "Mr Ingpen stated that Thomas gave him the manuscript of these poems just before leaving England for the Front. It is generally said that the book was in the press when Thomas was killed in France, 9 April 1917." (Eckert, p.242) When *Poems* appeared, there was a dedication after the title page: "To Robert Frost". This was the first book ever dedicated to him.

March

Now I know that Spring will come again,
Perhaps tomorrow: however late I've patience
After this night following on such a day.

While still my temples ached from the cold burning
Of hail and wind, and still the primroses
Torn by the hail were covered up in it,
The sun filled earth and heaven with a great light
And a tenderness, almost warmth, where the hail dripped,
As if the mighty sun wept tears of joy.
But 'twas too late for warmth. The sunset piled
Mountains on mountains of snow and ice in the west:
Somewhere among their folds the wind was lost,
And yet 'twas cold, and though I knew that Spring
Would come again, I knew it had not come,
That it was lost, too, in those mountains cold.

What did the thrushes know? Rain, snow, sleet, hail,
Had kept them quiet as the primroses.
They had but an hour to sing. On boughs they sang,
On gates, on ground; they sang while they changed
        perches
And while they fought, if they remembered to fight:
So earnest were they to pack into that hour
Their unwilling hoard of song before the moon
Grew brighter than the clouds. Then 'twas no time
For singing merely. So they could keep off silence
And night, they cared not what they sang or screamed,
Whether 'twas hoarse or sweet or fierce or soft,
And to me all was sweet: they could do no wrong.
Something they knew—I also, while they sang
And after. Not till night had half its stars
And never a cloud, was I aware of silence
Rich with all that riot of songs, a silence
Saying that Spring returns, perhaps tomorrow.

Old Man

Old Man, or Lad's-love,—in the name there's nothing
To one that knows not Lad's-love, or Old Man,
The hoar-green feathery herb, almost a tree,
Growing with rosemary and lavender.
Even to one that knows it well, the names
Half decorate, half perplex, the thing it is:
At least, what that is clings not to the names
In spite of time. And yet I like the names.

The herb itself I like not; but for certain
I love it, as some day the child will love it
Who plucks a feather from the door-side bush
Whenever she goes in or out of the house.
Often she waits there, snipping the tips and shrivelling
The shreds at last on to the path, perhaps
Thinking, perhaps of nothing, till she sniffs
Her fingers and runs off. The bush is still
But half as tall as she, though it is as old;
So well she clips it. Not a word she says;
And I can only wonder how much hereafter
She will remember, with that bitter scent,
Of garden rows, and ancient damson-trees
Topping a hedge, a bent path to a door,
A low thick bush beside the door, and me
Forbidding her to pick.
                                As for myself,
Where first I met the bitter scent is lost.
I, too, often shrivel the grey shreds,
Sniff them and think and sniff again and try
Once more to think what it is I am remembering,
Always in vain. I cannot like the scent,
Yet I would rather give up others more sweet,
With no meaning, than this bitter one.

I have mislaid the key. I sniff the spray
And think of nothing; I see and I hear nothing;

Yet seem, too, to be listening, lying in wait
For what I should, yet never can, remember:
No garden appears, no path, no hoar-green bush
Of Lad's-love, or Old Man, no child beside,
Neither father nor mother, nor any playmate;
Only an avenue, dark, nameless, without end.

The Combe

The Combe was ever dark, ancient and dark.
Its mouth is stopped with bramble, thorn, and briar;
And no one scrambles over the sliding chalk
By beech and yew and perishing juniper
Down the half precipices of its sides, with roots
And rabbit holes for steps. The sun of Winter,
The moon of Summer, and all the singing birds
Except the missel-thrush that loves juniper,
Are quite shut out. But far more ancient and dark
The Combe looks since they killed the badger there,
Dug him out and gave him to the hounds,
That most ancient Briton of English beasts.

Adlestrop

Yes, I remember Adlestrop—
The name, because one afternoon
Of heat the express-train drew up there
Unwontedly. It was late June.

The steam hissed. Someone cleared his throat.
No one left and no one came
On the bare platform. What I saw
Was Adlestrop—only the name

And willows, willow-herb, and grass,
And meadowsweet, and haycocks dry,
No whit less still and lonely fair
Than the high cloudlets in the sky.

And for that minute a blackbird sang
Close by, and round him, mistier,
Farther and farther, all the birds
Of Oxfordshire and Gloucestershire.

Fifty Faggots

There they stand, on their ends; the fifty faggots
That once were underwood of hazel and ash
In Jenny Pinks's Copse. Now, by the hedge
Close packed, they make a thicket fancy alone
Can creep through with the mouse and wren. Next Spring
A blackbird or robin will nest there,
Accustomed to them, thinking they will remain
Whatever is for ever to a bird:
This Spring it is too late; the swift has come.
'Twas a hot day for carrying them up:
Better they will never warm me, though they must
Light several Winters' fires. Before they are done
The war will have ended, many other things
Have ended, maybe, that I can no more
Foresee or more control than robin and wren.

The Sun Used to Shine

The sun used to shine while we two walked
Slowly together, paused and started
Again, and sometimes mused, sometimes talked
As either pleased, and cheerfully parted

Each night. We never disagreed
Which gate to rest on. The to be
And the late past we gave small heed.
We turned from men or poetry

To rumours of the war remote
Only till both stood disinclined
For aught but the yellow flavorous coat
Of an apple wasps had undermined;

Or a sentry of dark betonies,
The stateliest of small flowers on earth,
At the forest verge; or crocuses
Pale purple as if they had their birth

In sunless Hades fields. The war
Came back to mind with the moonrise
Which soldiers in the east afar
Beheld then. Nevertheless, our eyes

Could as well imagine the Crusades
Or Caesar's battles. Everything
To faintness like those rumours fades—
Like the brook's water glittering

Under the moonlight—like those walks
Now—like us two that took them, and
The fallen apples, all the talks
And silences—like memory's sand

When the tide covers it late or soon,
And other men through other flowers
In those fields under the same moon
Go talking and have easy hours.

A Dream [Sonnet 1]

Over known fields with an old friend in dream
I walked, but came sudden to a strange stream.
Its dark waters were bursting out most bright
From a great mountain's heart into the light.
They ran a short course under the sun, then back
Into a pit they plunged, once more as black
As at their birth: and I stood thinking there
How white, had the day shone on them, they were,
Heaving and coiling. So by the roar and hiss
And by the mighty motion of the abyss
I was bemused, that I forgot my friend
And neither saw nor sought him till the end,
When I awoke from waters unto men
Saying: 'I shall be here some day again.'

Aspens

All day and night, save winter, every weather,
Above the inn, the smithy, and the shop,
The aspens at the cross-roads talk together
Of rain, until their last leaves fall from the top.

Out of the blacksmith's cavern comes the ringing
Of hammer, shoe, and anvil; out of the inn
The clink, the hum, the roar, the random singing—
The sounds that for these fifty years have been.

The whisper of the aspens is not drowned,
And over lightless pane and footless road,
Empty as sky, with every other sound
Not ceasing, calls their ghosts from their abode,

A silent smith, a silent inn, nor fails
In the bare moonlight or the thick-furred gloom,
In tempest or the night of nightingales,
To turn the cross-roads to a ghostly room.

And it would be the same were no house near.
Over all sorts of weather, men, and times,
Aspens must shake their leaves and men may hear
But need not listen, more than to my rhymes.

Whatever wind blows, while they and I have leaves
We cannot other than an aspen be
That ceaselessly, unreasonably grieves,
Or so men think who like a different tree.

Words

Out of us all
That make rhymes,
Will you choose
Sometimes—
As the winds use
A crack in a wall
Or a drain,
Their joy or their pain
To whistle through—
Choose me,
You English words?

I know you:
You are light as dreams,
Tough as oak,
Precious as gold,
As poppies and corn,
Or an old cloak:
Sweet as our birds
To the ear,
As the burnet rose
In the heat
Of Midsummer:
Strange as the races
Of dead and unborn:
Strange and sweet
Equally,
And familiar,
To the eye,
As the dearest faces
That a man knows,
And as lost homes are:
But though older far
Than oldest yew,—
As our hills are, old,—
Worn new
Again and again;

Young as our streams
After rain:
And as dear
As the earth which you prove
That we love.

Make me content
With some sweetness
From Wales
Whose nightingales
Have no wings,—
From Wiltshire and Kent
And Herefordshire,
And the villages there,—
From the names, and the things
No less.

Let me sometimes dance
With you,
Or climb
Or stand perchance
In ecstasy,
Fixed and free
In a rhyme,
As poets do.

References

Books referred to by a shortened version in the text

Abercrombie, C.   Abercrombie, Mrs Lascelles: 'Memories of a Poet's Wife', *The Listener*, 15 November 1956, p.793

Anderson   Anderson, Margaret Bartlett: *Robert Frost and John Bartlett - The Record of a Friendship*, Holt, Rinehart & Winston, 1963

Brooke   Keynes, Geoffrey, ed: *The Letters of Rupert Brooke*, Faber and Faber, 1968

Clark   Clark, Keith: *The Muse Colony - Dymock 1914*, Redcliffe, 1992

Cooke   Cooke, William: *Edward Thomas: A Critical Biography*, Faber, 1970

Cooper   Private correspondence from Jeff Cooper (Abercrombie's grandson) to the author

Drinkwater, Inheritance   Drinkwater, John: *Inheritance, Being the First Book of an Autobiography*, Ernest Benn, 1931

Drinkwater, Discovery   Drinkwater, John: *Discovery, Being the Second Book of an Autobiography, 1897-1913*, Ernest Benn, 1932

Drinkwater   Drinkwater, John: *Rupert Brooke: An Essay*, printed for the author at Chiswick Press, 1916

Eckert   Eckert, Robert P.: *Edward Thomas - A Biography and a Bibliography*, J.M. Dent & Sons, 1937

Farjeon   Farjeon, Eleanor: *Edward Thomas - The Last Four Years*, Oxford University Press, 1979; revised edition, Sutton Publishing, 1997

Francis   Francis, Lesley Lee: *The Frost Family's Adventure in Poetry*, University of Missouri Press, 1994

Frost   Thompson, Lawrance, ed: *Selected Letters of Robert Frost*, Holt, Rinehart & Winston, 1964

Gawsworth   Gawsworth, John: *Ten Contemporaries: Notes Toward their Definitive Bibliography*, Ernest Benn, 1932

Gethyn-Jones   Gethyn-Jones, Rev. J.E.: *Dymock Down the Ages*, orig. 1951, reprinted Alan Sutton, 1985

Haines   Haines, John: 'Edward Thomas', *Gloucester Journal*, 16 February 1935

Hart   Hart, Linda: 'The Only Brother I Ever Had', *Acumen 30* (January 1998)

Hassall, Brooke   Hassall, Christopher: *Rupert Brooke: A Biography*, Faber and Faber, 1964

Hassall, Marsh   Hassall, Christopher: *Edward Marsh - Patron of the Arts*, Longmans, 1959

Marsh   Marsh, Jan: *Edward Thomas - A Poet for His Country*, Paul Elek, 1978

Marsh, Memoir Rupert Brooke: The Collected Poems with a memoir by Edward Marsh, Sidgwick & Jackson, 1918; 1979 edition.

Mertins   Mertins, Louis and Esther: *The Intervals of Robert Frost: A Critical Bibliography*, Russell & Russell, New York, 1947

Motion   Motion, Andrew: *The Poetry of Edward Thomas*, Routledge & Kegan Paul, 1980, republished Hogarth Press, 1991

Poetry Wales *Poetry Wales* - Edward Thomas Special Centenary Issue, Spring 1978, vol.13, no.4

Read   Read, Mike: *Forever England: The Life of Rupert Brooke*, Mainstream Publishing, 1997

Ross   Ross, Robert H.: *The Georgian Revolt: 1910-1922 - The Rise and Fall of a Poetic Ideal*, Southern Illinois University Press, 1965

Sergeant   Sergeant, Elizabeth: *Robert Frost: The Trial by Existence*, Holt, Rinehart and Winston, New York, 1960

Street   Street, Sean: *The Dymock Poets*, Seren, 1994

Thomas, Bottomley Thomas, R. George, ed: *Letters from Edward Thomas to Gordon Bottomley*, Oxford University Press, 1968

Thomas, Letters Thomas, R. George, ed: *Edward Thomas: Selected Letters*, Oxford University Press, 1995

Thomas, Poems Thomas, R. George, ed: *The Collected Poems of Edward Thomas*, Oxford University Press, 1978 [with interesting comments from Prof. Thomas about the origins of many of the poems]

Thomas, Sheaf Thomas, Edward: *The Last Sheaf: Essays by Edward Thomas*, Jonathan Cape, 1928

Thomas, Thomas Thomas, R. George, *Edward Thomas - A Portrait*, Clarendon Press, 1985

Turner   Turner, John Frayn: *Rupert Brooke - The Splendour and the Pain*, Breese Books, 1992

Walsh   Walsh, John Evangelist: *Into My Own - The English Years of Robert Frost*, Grove Weidenfeld, New York, 1988

Other books and articles

Armstrong, James & Linda Hart: *Robert Frost's Clouded Image*, Cheltenham & Gloucester College of Higher Education, Dymock Poets Archive & Study Centre, Occasional Paper no. 5, 1998

Berridge, Anthony, ed: *The Letters of Edward Thomas to Jesse Berridge*, Enitharmon Press, 1983

Cooper, Jeff: *Lascelles Abercrombie and the Origin of the Poets' Colony at Dymock*, Cheltenham & Gloucester College of Higher Education, Dymock Poets Archive & Study Centre, Occasional Paper no. 3, 1997

Coombes, H.: *Edward Thomas*, Chatto & Windus, 1956

Evans, William R.: *Robert Frost and Sidney Cox: Forty Years of Friendship*, University Press of New England, 1981

Haines, John: 'Wilfrid Gibson', Gloucester *Journal*, 15 December 1934; 'Lascelles Abercrombie', *Gloucester Journal*, 12 January 1935; 'Robert Frost', *Gloucester Journal*, 2 February 1935; 'Edward Thomas', *Gloucester Journal*, 16 February 1935;

_____ 'The Dymock Poets', *Gloucestershire Countryside*, October 1933 (vol 1, no 9, p.131)

Harvey, Anne, ed: *Elected Friends: Poems for and about Edward Thomas*, Enitharmon Press, 1991

Harvey, Anne, ed: *Adlestrop Revisited: An anthology inspired by Edward Thomas's poem*, Sutton Publishing, 1999

Meyers, Jeffrey: *Robert Frost: A biography*, Constable, 1996

Marsh, Edward, ed: *Georgian Poetry 1911-1912* and *Georgian Poetry 1913-1915*, The Poetry Bookshop, 1914 and 1918 respectively

Moore, John: *The Life and Letters of Edward Thomas*, Heinemann, 1939, republished Alan Sutton, 1983

Palmer, Roy: *The Folklore of Hereford and Worcester*, Logaston Press, 1992

Parini, Jay: *Robert Frost: A Life*, William Heinemann, 1998

Reeves, James, ed: *Georgian Poetry*, Penguin 1962, reprinted 1966

Rogers, Timothy, *Rupert Brooke: A Reappraisal and Selection*, Routledge & Kegan Paul, 1971

_____ ed: *Georgian Poetry 1911-1922: The Critical Heritage*, Routledge & Kegan Paul, 1977

Thomas, Edward: *In Pursuit of Spring*, Thomas Nelson & Sons 1914, reprinted Wildwood House, 1981

Thomas, Helen and Myfanwy: *Under Storm's Wing*, Paladin Books, 1990

Thomas, Edward: *Letters to Helen*, ed. R. George Thomas, Carcanet, 2000

Thompson, Lawrance: *Robert Frost: The Early Years 1894-1915*, Jonathan Cape, 1967.

Untermeyer, Louis, ed: *The Letters of Robert Frost to Louis Untermeyer*, Holt, Rinehart & Winston, New York, 1963

The poems have been taken from:

Abercrombie
New Numbers; *The Poems of Lascelles Abercrombie*, Oxford University Press, 1930

Brooke
New Numbers; *Rupert Brooke: The Collected Poems* - with a memoir by Edward Marsh, Sidgwick & Jackson, 1979

Drinkwater
New Numbers; *The Collected Poems of John Drinkwater*, vols I and II, Sidgwick & Jackson, 1923

Frost
The Poetry of Robert Frost - The Collected Poems Complete and Unabridged, edited by Edward Connery Lathem, Holt, Rinehart & Winston, 1969; and *Frost: Collected Poems, Prose, & Plays*, Library of America, 1995

Gibson
New Numbers; First editions of *Friends*, *Livelihood*, *Battle* and *The Golden Room*; *Collected Poems, 1905-1925*, Macmillan, 1929

Thomas
The Collected Poems of Edward Thomas, edited by R. George Thomas, Oxford University Press, 1978

Index

F

G

H

I

J

K

L

M